Conversations with Jack Kerouac

D0896809

Literary Conversations Series

Peggy Whitman Prenshaw
General Editor

Photo credit: courtesy Photofest

Conversations with Jack Kerouac

Edited by
Kevin J. Hayes

University Press of Mississippi
Jackson

www.upress.state.ms.us

The University Press of Mississippi is a member of the Association of American University Presses.

Copyright © 2005 by University Press of Mississippi
All rights reserved
Manufactured in the United States of America

13 12 11 10 09 08 07 06 05   4 3 2 1

∞

Library of Congress Cataloging-in-Publication Data

Conversations with Jack Kerouac / edited by Kevin J. Hayes.
    p. cm.
  Includes index.
  ISBN 1-57806-755-3 (cloth : alk. paper) — ISBN 1-57806-756-1 (pbk. : alk. paper)
  1. Kerouac, Jack, 1922–1969—Interviews. 2. Authors, American—20th century—Interviews. 3. Beat generation—Interviews. I. Hayes, Kevin J.

  PS3521.E735Z625   2005
  813'.54—dc22   2004026277

British Library Cataloging-in-Publication Data available

Books by Jack Kerouac

The Town and the City. New York: Harcourt, Brace, 1950.

On the Road. New York: Viking, 1957.

The Subterraneans. New York: Grove, 1958.

The Dharma Bums. New York: Viking, 1958.

Doctor Sax: Faust Part Three. New York: Grove, 1959.

Maggie Cassidy. New York: Avon, 1959.

Mexico City Blues. New York: Grove, 1959.

Excerpts From Visions of Cody. New York: New Directions, 1960.

The Scripture of the Golden Eternity. New York: Totem Press/Corinth Books, 1960.

Tristessa. New York: Avon, 1960.

Lonesome Traveler. New York: McGraw-Hill, 1960.

Book of Dreams. San Francisco: City Lights Books, 1961.

Pull My Daisy. New York: Grove, 1961.

Big Sur. New York: Farrar, Straus & Cudahy, 1962.

Visions of Gerard. New York: Farrar, Straus, 1963.

Desolation Angels. New York: Coward-McCann, 1965.

Satori in Paris. New York: Grove, 1966.

Vanity of Duluoz: An Adventurous Education 1935–46. New York: Coward-McCann, 1968.

Scattered Poems. San Francisco: City Lights Books, 1971.

Pic. New York: Grove, 1971.

Visions of Cody. New York: McGraw-Hill, 1972.

With Albert Saijo and Lew Welch. *Trip Trap. Haiku along the Road from San Francisco to New York, 1959*. Bolinas, CA: Grey Fox Press, 1973.

Heaven and Other Poems. Bolinas, CA: Grey Fox, 1977.

San Francisco Blues. N.p.: Beat Books, 1983.

Good Blonde and Others, ed. Donald Allen. San Francisco: Grey Fox, 1993.

Old Angel Midnight, ed. Donald Allen. San Francisco: Grey Fox Press, 1993.

Book of Blues. New York: Penguin, 1995.

Selected Letters, 1940–1956, ed. Ann Charters. New York: Viking, 1995.

Some of the Dharma. New York: Viking, 1997.

Atop an Underwood: Early Stories and Other Writings, ed. Paul Marion. New York: Viking, 1999.

Selected Letters, 1957–1969, ed. Ann Charters. New York: Viking, 1999.

Book of Haikus, ed. Regina Weinreich. New York: Penguin Poets, 2003.

Contents

Introduction ix

Chronology xix

Mike Wallace Asks Jack Kerouac: What Is the Beat Generation?
Mike Wallace 3

On the Road Back: How the Beat Generation Got That Way, According to
Its Seer *Anonymous* 7

St. Jack (Annotated by Jack Kerouac) *Al Aronowitz* 10

What Is the Beat Generation? *Val Duncan* 37

Playing "Baseball" with Jack Kerouac *Stan Isaacs* 40

I Simply Plan a Completely Written Lifetime *Anonymous* 43

Kerouac Revisited *Val Duncan* 46

The Art of Fiction: Jack Kerouac *Ted Berrigan* 51

Off the Road: The Celtic Twilight of Jack Kerouac
Gregory McDonald 82

Jack Kerouac Is on the Road No More *Jack McClintock* 91

Index 97

Introduction

One Saturday morning back in the late seventies when I was in college, a friend and fellow classmate of mine at the University of Toledo popped over unexpectedly. She told me she was going to Ann Arbor to shop for used books and asked me if I wanted to come along. Having never been shopping for used books in Ann Arbor, I readily agreed. Seeing what she was driving—an aquamarine '58 Rambler—I began to have second thoughts. That car's older than I am, I thought. Still, I accepted my lot, climbed into the passenger seat, and, by reflex, looked for the seatbelt. My search was in vain.

"There are no seatbelts in this car," I observed.

"Yes, does that bother you?" she asked.

"No," I lied.

"People didn't worry about safety back then," she told me. "They just drove for fun."

That car was older than she was, too, so I'm unsure how much I believed what she was saying, but I changed the subject, and we began talking of other things.

By this point in our conversation, we had reached Alexis Road. It has always thrilled me that this, one of the principle east-west roads through our city, was named for the patron saint of hermits and beggars. Alexis brought us to U.S. 23. The Rambler took the numerous potholes on 23 like a trooper, and we made it safely to Ann Arbor in less than an hour.

Slotting the Rambler into a parking space in the multi-level garage adjacent to Jacobson's Department Store, we made our way down to street level, through Nickels Arcade, and onto State Street, where the finest secondhand bookstore in town, the aptly-named State Street Bookshop, was located. The reputation of this shop was based on both its selection and its clear organization. Hardbacks, organized by subject and alphabetized within each subject, were up front. Paperbacks, also organized by subject and alphabetized within the subject, were located in back.

I headed toward the section devoted to paperback fiction. Looking for one novel in particular, Ken Kesey's *Sometimes a Great Notion*, I directed my eyes to the "k" shelf. Kesey was nowhere in sight, so I started browsing to see if I could find anything else interesting. On the shelf where Kesey should have been I spied a book I had never heard of by an author I had never heard of. The author was Jack Kerouac, and the book was *On the Road*. Given my interest in American literature and adventuresome travel, *On the Road* seemed to offer ideal reading. I bought it, read it, and found it delightful. Little did I realize that *On the Road* would lead me on a literary journey that would span decades.

After reading *On the Road*, I had an urge to read anything and everything by Jack Kerouac. Satisfying this urge was not as easy as it seemed and certainly not as easy as it is now. By the late seventies, most of Kerouac's novels had gone out of print. I started my search for other Kerouac books at Carlson Library, the main library at the University of Toledo. Though the card catalog held records for several Kerouac titles, few of the recorded titles were in the stacks. I asked the librarian at the circulation counter where they were. She informed me that the absent books were not checked out and concluded that they must have been stolen.

Frustrated but undaunted, I headed to the downtown Toledo Public Library next. Here, I found a few Kerouac books but far fewer than I had expected. Conveniently, the card catalog at the downtown library contained records of the holdings of all of the branch libraries in the metropolitan area, so I made of a list of what libraries had which books and pedaled my powder-blue Schwinn Continental around town as I tried to track down Kerouac. At one neighborhood library after another, my experience was much the same. Copies of Kerouac had been stolen from each library I visited.

It says something about an author that his works inspire such thievery among his readers. The theft of Kerouac books, I now conclude, has two principle causes. Generally speaking, his works advocate an alternative lifestyle. Kerouac stands against the establishment, against the middle class values that the neighborhood public library represents. According to the lifestyle his writings inspire, minor deviations from established norms of behavior are acceptable if they can be justified by the greater good of heightening the consciousness of the individual.

The other reason why so many copies of Kerouac were stolen has less to do with their texts and more to do with the power of books to transcend the texts they contain. Like those of any author who develops a cult following, Kerouac's books have assumed the quality of magic talismans. Borrowing his books from the public library is not enough for his most enthusiastic followers. For the true Kerouac devotee, owning his books becomes important, too, more important than obeying laws prohibiting theft. Possessing a tattered copy of, say, *The Dharma Bums*, is something like owning a piece of the true cross. The epithet often used to describe Kerouac's most famous work reinforces its talismanic status: *On the Road* is known as the Bible of the Beat Generation.

Val Duncan, a reporter for *Newsday* who interviewed Kerouac at two different times in his career, coined a different epithet for *On the Road*. Duncan called it the "Baedeker of Beatism." Making reference to the longstanding series of popular travel guides, Duncan's phrase reinforces the ways in which *On the Road* functions. The work's text guides readers toward a particular outlook on life. Carried on the person, it functions as a good luck charm to assure them they will be able to reach their destination safely. Duncan coined the epithet in his 1959 interview, but it still applied two decades later when I first read *On the Road*. And, for many Kerouac enthusiasts, it still applies today. To young adults with a dual interest in literature and adventure, *On the Road* remains a Baedeker of the mind.

Since the local libraries in Toledo were unable to quench my newfound thirst for Kerouac's writings, I made my way back to the secondhand bookshops in Ann Arbor. *The Dharma Bums*, even more than *On the Road*, became my Baedeker, but I did not stop there. *The Subterraneans, Desolation Angels, Visions of Cody, Lonesome Traveler*: all became a part of my personal library and helped to shape my personal outlook.

Combing Ann Arbor one day for a few of the Kerouac books I had yet to read—*Dr. Sax, Visions of Gerard*—I was thwarted in my quest. This day I almost left Ann Arbor empty-handed, but on my way out of the State Street Bookshop, I happened to find on the sale table near the door a volume of interviews reprinted from *The Paris Review* "Writers at Work" series. The collection contained a lengthy interview with Jack Kerouac. Having read all the Kerouac I could find, this, the classic Kerouac interview, proved a boon to the personal program of reading he had inspired. After digesting this interview, I shifted from reading what Kerouac had written to reading what he had read. His enthusiasm for Balzac, Proust, and many other authors gave me new suggestions for reading that would take years to fulfill.

Reading Kerouac's *Paris Review* interview, I received an object lesson in the value of literary interviews. A single interview provides a glimpse into an author's mind at a particular point in time. The interview can reveal what thrills them, what scares them, what drives them. Read together, a series of interviews conducted over a career shows how a writer's thrills, fears, and drives change over the course of time. Such is the intended purpose of the present collection.

The funny shape of Kerouac's literary career lends a funny shape to his interviews. His first novel, *The Town and the City*, generated little attention when it appeared in 1950, and seven years passed before his second novel, *On the Road*, appeared to instant acclaim and established Kerouac's renown as the voice of a new generation. In that seven-year period, Kerouac wrote the bulk of his oeuvre. Though he had difficulty finding a publisher for *On the Road*, he was not discouraged from writing other novels. Having developed his spontaneous prose style during the composition of this novel, he continued to apply it to many other works he composed before *On the Road* was published. By the time interviewers began hounding him in the late 1950s, Kerouac's most fruitful artistic period had already passed.

His first major, national interview occurred on television. Shortly after *On the Road* exploded onto the literary scene, he was scheduled to appear on John Wingate's *Nightbeat* in September 1957. No complete transcript of the interview survives, but Kerouac made multiple references to it in his correspondence, as Ann Charters's fine two-volume edition of his letters shows. Other scattered references to the *Nightbeat* interview survive, too. In a letter to Allen Ginsberg shortly after the interview, Kerouac described the evening as a "mad night" and explained that in responding to Wingate's "evil questions," he had "answered angelic." In a letter to Neal Cassady, Kerouac suggested that his unexpected answers had "Wingate fluttering thru his prepared questions sweating." By accounts other than his own, Kerouac gave a disastrous performance before the television cameras. To many of Wingate's questions he said nothing. The frenetic voice that leaps from the pages of *On the Road* was silenced in person.

Interviewing Kerouac for *The Village Voice* shortly after the *Nightbeat* interview, Jerry Tallmer chose a much more amenable location, Goody's Bar in Greenwich Village. With the Schlitz flowing, Tallmer got Kerouac to open up about the *Nightbeat* interview and also coaxed additional information from him about his life and work. Tallmer captured Kerouac's personal

allure, calling him even more handsome than Cary Grant. In conversation
with Tallmer, Kerouac spoke of his love of jazz, his experience on the West
Coast with Kenneth Rexroth, and his composition of *Dr. Sax*.

If Kerouac thought his tough interviews were over once he had finished
Nightbeat, then he was sadly mistaken. In January 1958, he faced none other
than Mike Wallace, who has made hard-hitting interviews the defining fea-
ture of his journalistic career. When *Sixty Minutes* was at its muckraking
peak in the 1970s, a joke circulated among business owners: "You know it's
going to be a bad day when Mike Wallace comes to your door." Wallace's 1958
interview with Kerouac shows that he had already developed his interviewing
style by the time he met this "King of the Beats."

Though less sympathetic than Val Duncan, Wallace had much the same
intention, to define the Beat Generation and to determine what its members
represented. Trying to pin down the meaning of the word "Beat," Wallace
grilled Kerouac, interrogating his religious views, his drug use, his attitude
toward death and the afterlife, and even his personal happiness.

In 1959, Al Aronowitz, also seeking to define the Beat Generation but
going about it with more patience, was doing a series of articles on the Beat
Generation. Naturally enough, he decided to interview Kerouac at the home
in Northport, Long Island where he lived with his mother. The interview
lasted a full two hours, and Aronowitz tape-recorded the whole thing. He
later submitted the article to Kerouac, who provided him with many additional comments in follow-up letters. An abbreviated version of this interview appeared in the *New York Post* as part of the series, but the complete
interview, annotated by Aronowitz with excerpts from Kerouac's unpublished
letters to him, has only appeared previously in a limited, photocopied edition. With its length and its early date—several years before the other long
interviews of Kerouac, Aronowitz's interview offers a unique glimpse into
Kerouac's life and thought. Kerouac shared with Aronowitz scrapbooks of his
younger days and notebooks containing much of his unpublished work. He
talked about old times in New York; his periodical publications; his attitude
toward English prose; his life in California; *Book of Dreams*, a work in
progress nightly; his dissatisfaction with copy editors; Henry Miller, who had
agreed to write a preface for *The Subterraneans*; his appreciation of Neal
Cassady; and what may be the most fascinating comment in the interview, a
comparison between the interview as it is taking place and the interviews that
structure *Citizen Kane*.

Upon making the comparison, Kerouac elaborated what he meant: "Remember the guy in *Citizen Kane* going around, getting all this, seeing old Joseph Cotten at the hospital. That's me. Then he goes to see the old Jewish publisher, remember that? Everett Sloane. There was a guy going around— who was it? You know when I saw it? I saw it Pearl Harbor day. I came out of the theater and saw the headlines about Pearl Harbor. It was a Sunday night." Kerouac's analogy essentially splits himself in two. The newspaper reporter in *Citizen Kane* interviewing Jedediah Leland, the character played by Joseph Cotten, is seeking information about Charlie Kane. Al Aronowitz interviewed Jack Kerouac seeking information about Jack Kerouac. The analogy suggests that Kerouac saw himself as two different people: "Jack Kerouac," the Beat writer who had caught the attention of the reading public, and Jack Kerouac, the private man who had matured beyond the adventures his books narrated and lived in quiet seclusion with his widowed mother.

The analogy to *Citizen Kane* also conveys the impossibility of getting to know anyone solely by means of an interview. From each interviewee the reporter in the film obtains a partial glimpse of his subject, never the complete picture, never the true picture. The interviews with Kerouac over the course of his career have much the same effect.

Kerouac's reference to *Citizen Kane* in conversation with Aronowitz also says something about his storytelling ability and, in so doing, sheds light on his creativity. In his interviews, Kerouac stressed the autobiographical nature of his fiction, emphasizing that the stories he told were true and only the names had been changed. Answers to interview questions are also a form of autobiography, presumably true stories of what happened. Telling Aronowitz that he had seen *Citizen Kane* the night of December 7, 1941, however, Kerouac deliberately lied. His correspondence indicates that he had already seen it by then. Besides, nowhere in New York City was *Citizen Kane* playing that night. Kerouac deliberately refashioned his story to make it more dramatic.

Kerouac himself recognized the similarity between his answers to interviewers' questions and his own writings. In the *Paris Review* interview, he compared the interview-as-genre with his own work: "I am so busy interviewing myself in my novels, and have been so busy writing down these self-interviews, that I don't see why I should draw breath in pain every year of the last ten years to repeat and repeat to everybody who interviews me what I've already explained in the books themselves." He had already told stories of his past the way he wanted to tell them. He saw no particular reason to retell them in a different form, that is, as answers to questions recorded on tape. In a way, he had already progressed beyond the tape recording as a medium for verbal expression.

In the early fifties, even before he completed *On the Road*. Kerouac had experimented with a tape recorder and taped three nights of conversations between himself and Neal Cassady. Kerouac transcribed these recordings and incorporated them into *Visions of Cody*. In his introduction to the unexpurgated *Visions of Cody* first published three years after Kerouac's death, Allen Ginsberg made the case for these taped conversations. Kerouac's transcription of these recordings is art, Ginsberg argued, because it marks a particular point in the development of his literary aesthetic, a time when he "began transcribing *first* thoughts of true mind in American speech." Kerouac's transcription of these tape recordings represents a point of transition between the mannered literary style of *The Town and the City* and the spontaneous prose style of *On the Road* and virtually every work Kerouac wrote afterwards.

Recalling his experiences with the tape recorder in the *Paris Review* interview, Kerouac commented, "I haven't used this method since; it really doesn't come out right, well, with Neal and with myself, when all written down and with all the Ahs and the Ohs and the Ahums and the fearful fact that the damn thing is turning and you're *forced* not to waste electricity or tape."

Though the tape recorder may have considerable limitations as an artistic medium for creating literature, as a medium for doing documentary work it is surpassed only by motion pictures. And none of Kerouac's interviewers used the tape recorder more fully than did Miklos Zsedely, associate librarian at the Northport Public Library. Zsedely arranged an interview with Kerouac and a group of his friends at the studio of Long Island artist Stanley Twardowicz as part of the library's local oral history project. Currently, the recording is available at the Northport Public Library, where anyone with several hours to spare can listen to it.

The three principle figures in the conversation are Twardowicz, Kerouac, and Jim Schwaner, a self-proclaimed philosopher and quondam bartender. Zsedely himself seems at somewhat of a loss as to how to deal with these competing voices and, for the most part, lets the conversation go where it will. Describing the transcriptions of tape recordings that appear in *Visions of Cody*, Ginsberg characterized them as "unaltered and unadorned—halts, switches, emptiness, quixotic chatters, summary piths, exactly reproduced." Much the same description applies to Zsedely's Northport interview.

In the first third of the interview, Kerouac is fairly quiet as Schwaner and Twardowicz dominate the conversation. Partway through the evening, they run out of beer and must stop tape to go out for more. At this point, Schwaner goes home. The beer supply restocked, the interview continues. With Schwaner's departure, the interview becomes much more intimate, and Kerouac's voice emerges. Still, the interview yields few insights in relation to its profound length. It is best presented by way of abstract:

> On the spontaneous artistic style of Franz Kline versus his own spontaneous prose style: "He doesn't go as far as I do. I have to go on all night; he just goes ftch ftch ftch and he's finished. . . . However, the Japanese brush painters did that. They spent six months thinking, then they went fsht fsht fsht fsht fsht then they had a tiger in the bamboo."
>
> On Dean Moriarity's exit in *On the Road*: "When you last see him he's twinkling away like Charlie Chaplin."
>
> On Shakespeare: "The greatest poet that shall ever live, ever did, does, and ever shall."
>
> On Norman Mailer: "I would say 'hipster' [instead of beatnik]. Now the reason why I can't say 'hipster' is because Mailer jumped on that. Mailer. 'Kerouac is a beatnik and I'm a hipster.' He's a hipster 'cause he goes to boxing matches. And then he has a picture taken of him in *Esquire* magazine, standing in a corner ready to take on any American novelist. I'm telling you, if he ever wants to have a fight with me, I'd get mad."
>
> On modern American writers: "The nineteenth-century American writers were much greater. There's only one twentieth-century American writer who could compare to Melville, Whitman—Wolfe."
>
> On the reason for existence: "God wanted to amuse himself with a movie. You know, to watch a movie! God's watchin' us. A funny movie."

Kerouac traveled to France in 1965. The trip provided the experiences that resulted in *Satori in Paris*. In my personal quest to read everything Kerouac wrote, I distinctly remember reading *Satori in Paris*, which soured me on Kerouac for a long time. *The Dharma Bums* had prompted me to learn more about Buddhism, and ever since reading that book, the concept of satori had intrigued me. This new book seemed like a travesty. As near as I could tell, it had nothing to do with satori. The novel seemed to present little more than a minor episode in the life of a pitiful, self-centered, cranky drunk.

The last two interviews in this collection present a similar impression. Interviewing Kerouac in Lowell shortly before he, his wife Stella, and his mother moved to St. Petersburg, Florida, Gregory MacDonald captured Kerouac's pitiful existence during the final two years of his life. Seated in his favorite rocking chair and wearing pajama bottoms and a flannel shirt that did nothing to mask his big gut, Kerouac rocks back and forth, drinking and watching daytime television. In this interview, Kerouac conveyed his hope for getting a big advance on his next project, a hope that everyone can tell is a lost one save for Kerouac himself. Furthermore, he expressed bitterness toward the hippie movement, which his works had helped to spawn. By late afternoon, he was ready to hit the bars, so MacDonald agreed to accompany him. Loud and obnoxious, Kerouac recited lines from Emily Dickinson at one bar after another. Macdonald finally left him after Kerouac passed out at the last bar.

The interview conducted by Jack McClintock in St. Petersburg, Kerouac's last interview, appeared nine days before he died of internal hemorrhaging caused by years of alcohol abuse, and anticipated his death, both in its title and its contents. Telling McClintock that he had "a goddam hernia," Kerouac nevertheless drank multiple shots of scotch chased with Falstaff tallboys over the course of the interview.

The tragedy of Jack Kerouac is not that he drank himself to death. The tragedy of Jack Kerouac is that he let his art stagnate. In *System and Dialectics of Art* (1937), John Graham had emphasized the importance of risk, accident, and self-indulgence for generating artistic expression. In art, Jackson Pollock came to exemplify the ideas Graham advanced. In music, jazz improvisation was one manifestation of such ideas. In literature, Kerouac's spontaneous prose style, which was directly inspired by jazz improvisation, represents the literary manifestation of what Graham articulated. Kerouac is important to the history of American literature and culture for embodying the spirit of the Beat Generation in his writings and for perpetuating the longstanding tradition of American restlessness. He is important to the history of literary discourse for developing his spontaneous prose style. Having invented the spontaneous style, however, Kerouac never progressed beyond it.

One reason why he never developed further in terms of his writing style is because of the limitations he deliberately imposed on himself. "Duluoz" was one name he invented for his fictional persona, and "Legend of Duluoz" was the phrase he coined to describe his oeuvre. As he told an anonymous interviewer upon the publication of *Visions of Gerard*, he designed his oeuvre as "a completely written lifetime with all its hundreds of characters and events and levels interswirling and reappearing and becoming complete, somewhat a la Balzac and Proust."

There is a key difference between Balzac's *Comédie Humaine* and Kerouac's "Legend of Duluoz." Conceiving his oeuvre, Balzac imagined a fictional world that spanned many generations of many families and crossed different geographical and social barriers. Conceiving his oeuvre, Kerouac imagined it as an extended, multi-volume autobiography. Consequently, his scope was much more limited. Furthermore, Kerouac's concept made his art directly dependent on his life. His art stagnated because his life stagnated. In the late forties through the mid fifties, Kerouac had enough exciting personal experiences to fill several novels. In the sixties, as the late interviews suggest, he was little more than an unshaven, middle-aged drunk in a tattered bathrobe and worn house slippers: a good character for an Edward Albee play but hardly an ideal protagonist for a dynamic novel.

Sadly, Kerouac never realized the limitation of the "Legend of Duluoz" in terms of either style, subject, or genre. He never reached the point where he said, "O.K., the legend is played out. I need to reconceive my oeuvre." The shame is that he could have. He had it in him. Consider the essays that comprise *Lonesome Traveler*. They show that he had the capacity to turn essayist. Or consider the imaginative possibilities of the fantasy baseball game he invented.

In a 1961 interview with *Newsday* sports commentator Stan Isaacs, Kerouac demonstrated the solitaire baseball card game he invented to while away the long, tedious hours as a fire lookout atop Desolation Peak. He demonstrated to Isaacs how the game worked over the course of nine full innings. The interview originally appeared on the sports page and even included a box score. Each fictional team has a full complement of players, and every player has a personality of his own. The interview shows the sheer power of Kerouac's memory and the fertility of his imagination. The creativity displayed with this fantasy baseball game Kerouac never really applied to his writing. Once he embraced spontaneity—not only as an aesthetic approach but also as a lifestyle—he found it impossible to abandon.

KJH

Chronology

1922   On March 12, Jack Kerouac is born in Lowell, Massachusetts, the third child of Leo and Gabrielle Kerouac.

1926   Jack's brother Gerard dies from rheumatic fever.

1939   Kerouac graduates from Lowell High School, where he has distinguished himself as a football player. In the fall he begins attending the Horace Mann School in New York to prepare for his admission to Columbia the following year.

1940   In September, Kerouac matriculates at Columbia University on a football scholarship but breaks his leg during a football game in October.

1941   Kerouac leaves Columbia in the fall.

1942   Kerouac joins the merchant marines and sails to Greenland.

1943   Enlisting in the Navy in February, Kerouac is discharged in September. After a brief trip to Liverpool, he returns to New York by year's end.

1944   Kerouac meets William Burroughs, Allen Ginsberg, and Herbert Huncke. In August, he and Edie Parker marry; the marriage would be annulled less than two years later.

1946   Kerouac begins writing *The Town and the City*. His father dies of stomach cancer. In December Kerouac meets Neal Cassady.

1947   Cassady leaves New York in March. In July Kerouac takes a bus to Denver, a journey marking the start of the adventures he would chronicle in *On the Road*. From Denver he makes his way to California, returning to New York in October.

1949   Early this year, Kerouac takes another trip across the continent to California and back.

1950   Harcourt, Brace publishes *The Town and the City*. Kerouac meets Neal Cassady in Denver and together they drive to Mexico City, where they visit William Burroughs. In mid year, he leaves Mexico for New York, where he meets and marries Joan Haverty.

1951   Kerouac writes *On the Road*. He and Joan separate, unaware she is
        pregnant with daughter Jan, who would be born in February the
        following year.

1952   Kerouac divides much of his time this year between California and
        Mexico, where he writes *Dr. Sax*. He ends the year back in New
        York.

1953   Kerouac writes *Maggie Cassidy* and *The Subterraneans*.

1954   In January Kerouac hitchhikes from New York to California, where
        he becomes interested in Buddhism. He returns to the East Coast
        but his phlebitis makes it difficult for him to find work, and he is
        arrested for non-support of his daughter.

1955   In August, Kerouac hitchhikes to Mexico City, where he writes
        Mexico City Blues and has the experiences that inspire *Tristessa*.
        Later in the year, he travels to the San Francisco Bay area to see
        Ginsberg. Here he meets Lawrence Ferlinghetti, Kenneth Rexroth,
        Gary Snyder, and Philip Whalen. With Snyder, he climbs the 12,000
        foot high Matterhorn mountain in the Sierra Nevada chain in
        October. In December, he visits his sister in Rocky Mount, North
        Carolina, where he writes *Visions of Gerard*.

1956   Kerouac returns to California in April, where he shares a cabin
        with Gary Snyder. In June he hitchhikes north to Washington to
        take a job as a fire lookout atop Desolation Peak in the Cascades. In
        September he returns to Mexico City, where he completes *Tristessa*
        and begins *Desolation Angels*.

1957   In February, Kerouac leaves New York to see William Burroughs in
        Tangier and ends up typing the manuscript of Burroughs's *Naked
        Lunch*. From Tangier, Kerouac travels through France and England.
        Viking publishes *On the Road* the first week of September to
        instant acclaim. The book established Kerouac's reputation as the
        leader of the Beat movement. In November, he begins writing *The
        Dharma Bums*.

1958   *The Subterraneans* appears in February. In March Kerouac pur-
        chases a house in Northport, Long Island, the first of several homes
        he would own there, as he and his mother vacillate between Long
        Island and Florida over the next several years. In October, *The
        Dharma Bums* appears and further solidifies Kerouac's literary
        reputation.

1959   *Doctor Sax* appears in April, *Maggie Cassidy* in July, and *Mexico City Blues* in November.

1960   *Tristessa* and *Visions of Cody* appear in June. *Lonesome Traveler* is published in September and *Book of Dreams* in December.

1962   *Big Sur* appears in September.

1963   *Visions of Gerard* appears in September.

1964   Neal Cassady, now driving the bus for Ken Kesey's Merry Pranksters, introduces Kerouac to them. Kerouac sells his final home in Northport, moving back to Florida.

1965   *Desolation Angels* appears in May. Kerouac visits Paris briefly in June, the journey that would inspire *Satori in Paris*.

1966   Kerouac and his mother move from Florida to Hyannis, on Cape Cod. Grove Press publishes *Satori in Paris*. In November, Kerouac weds Stella Sampas in Hyannis.

1967   In January, the Kerouacs move to Lowell.

1968   Kerouac learns of Neal Cassady's death in February. *Vanity of Duluoz* is published this month. Kerouac travels to Europe with Tony and Nick Sampas. The Kerouacs move to St. Petersburg, Florida.

1969   On October 21, Kerouac dies in St. Petersburg, Florida, from internal hemorrhaging brought about by excessive drinking. He was forty-seven.

Conversations with Jack Kerouac

Mike Wallace Asks Jack Kerouac: What Is the Beat Generation?

Mike Wallace / 1958

From *New York Post*, January 21, 1958, p. 16. Reprinted with permission from the NEW YORK POST, © 1958, NYP Holdings, Inc.

In twentieth century America, a new kind of mystic has appeared—the Beat Generation visionary. He doesn't eat locusts, wear hair shirts, sleep on nails or perch on pillars. He uses the strange modern techniques of jive, junk and high speed to achieve his special ecstasy. Here we interview Jack Kerouac, author of *On the Road* and chronicler of the Beat Generation. A tattered, forlorn young man, with the chronic exhaustion of one who eats and sleeps infrequently, Kerouac gives us a glimmering of the hope and despair of the Beat in their search for the Beatitudes.

Q: What is the Beat Generation?
A: Well, actually it's just an old phrase. I knocked it off one day and they made a big fuss about it. It's not really a generation at all.

Q: It's a type of person?
A: Yeah. It starts with rock 'n' roll teenagers and runs up to sixty-year-old junkies, old characters in the street. . . . It really began in 1910.

Q: Well, what links the junkie and the fourteen-year-old and Jack Kerouac? What is it to be Beat?
A: Well, it's a hipness. It's twentieth century hipness.

Q: Hip to what?
A: To life.

Q: What kind of life are they hip to?
A: . . . to religion.

Q: What kind of religion?
A: Oh, it's weird. Visions. Visions of God.

Q: You mean Beat people are mystics?
A: Yeah. It's a revival prophesied by Spengler. He said that in the late moments of Western civilization there would be a great revival of religious mysticism. It's happening.

Q: What sort of mysticism is it? What do Beat mystics believe in?
A: Oh, they believe in love. They love children . . . and I don't know; it's so strange to talk about all this . . . they love children, they love women, they love animals, they love everything.

Q: They love everything? Then why is there so much violence? Why do they drive, drive, drive? Why do they go, go, go? Why the rush?
A: Oh, that's just lyricism. Wild motorcycle rides under the moonlight . . . A lyrical thing. It's not so unusual.

Q: Why is jazz so important to this new mysticism?
A: That's the music of the Beat Generation.

Q: What's mystical about it?
A: Jazz is very complicated. It's just as complicated as Bach. The chords, the structures, the harmony and everything. And then it has a tremendous beat. You know, tremendous drummers. They can drive it. It has just a tremendous drive. It can drive you right out of yourself.

Q: How about dope?
A: Same thing. You can escape. You can have visions with dope.

Q: Have you ever taken dope yourself?
A: Sure. A lot. But I never got in the habit because I'm allergic to it.

Q: Have you had visions with it?
A: I'll say.

Q: Do you remember any clearly?
A: I fainted. I passed out, fell flat on my back on the grass. During that time, I saw Paradise, I saw—well, I wasn't there any more. There was only one thing . . . there was a great golden light, and I wasn't there . . . but it was like, I suppose, God . . . But it was so blissful, because I didn't have to worry about being myself anymore. That was all over with . . .

Q: Sounds like a self-destructive way to seek God.
A: Oh, it was tremendous. I woke up sick about the fact that I had to come back to myself, to the flesh of life . . .

Q: You mean that the Beat people want to lose themselves?
A: Yeah. You know, Jesus said to see the Kingdom of Heaven you must lose yourself . . . something like that.

Q: Then the Beat Generation loves death?
A: Yeah. They're not afraid of death.

Q: Aren't you afraid?
A: Naw . . . What I believe is that nothing is happening.

Q: What do you mean?
A: Well, you're not sitting here. That's what you *think.* Actually, we are great empty space. I could walk right *through* you . . . You know what I mean, we're made out of atoms, electrons. We're actually empty. We're an empty vision . . . in one mind.

Q: In what mind—the mind of God?
A: That's the name we give it. We can give it any name. We can call it tangerine . . . god . . . tangerine . . . But I do know we are empty phantoms, sitting here thinking we are human beings and worrying about civilization. We're just empty phantoms. And yet, all is well.

Q: All is well?
A: Yeah. We're all in Heaven, now, really.

Q: You don't *sound* happy.
A: Oh, I'm tremendously sad. I'm in great despair.

Q: Why?
A: It's a great burden to be alive. A heavy burden, a great big heavy burden. I wish I were safe in Heaven, dead.

Q: But you *are* in Heaven, Jack. You just said we all were.
A: Yeah. If I only *knew* it. If I could only hold on to what I *know*.

"You must meet my friend, Philip Lamantia," said Kerouac casually on departing. "He was knocked off a bench by an angel last week."

On the Road Back: How the Beat Generation Got That Way, According to Its Seer

Anonymous / 1958

From *San Francisco Examiner*, October 5, 1958, *Highlight* sec. p. 18. Reprinted with permission.

Drum major for the beat generation, setting the wild, free, jazz tempo by which it marches out of step with society, is Jack Kerouac, a one time San Franciscan who now lives on Long Island. His novels about the hopped up, way out, nomadic cool cats of that generation, *On the Road* and *The Subterraneans*, have excited both cheers and boos from the critics, and a hubbub of controversy throughout the Nation. Kerouac's latest novel, *The Dharma Bums*, is reviewed in this section. Here he answers some questions fired by *Highlight*:

Q: Would you tell us your version of the origin of the term "beat generation" and why San Francisco happens to be its most fertile ground for growth?
A: In 1948 I said to John Clellon Holmes, "This is really a beat generation." He agreed and in 1952 published an article in the *New York Times* entitled "This Is the Beat Generation" and attributed the original vision to me.

Also, I had already called it the Beat Generation in my manuscript of *On the Road* written in May 1951. San Francisco is the last great city in America, after that no more land. It was there where poets and bums could come and drink wine in the streets before the recent crackdown by police who spend too much time watching *San Francisco Beat* on TV and not enough time reading books in the library.

Q: What would you say is the chief difference, if any between the "lost" generation of Fitzgerald-Hemingway and the "beat" generation of today?
A: The Lost Generation, from what I can tell from the books, was based on an ironic romantic negation. "Beat" generation is sweating for affirmation,

7

and yet there is an irony, almost a cynicism, involved, a kind of lip-service about the "greatness" of life. And, of course, Romanticism is dead: In its place, the search for gnosticism, absolute belief in a Divinity of Rapture. I believe God is Ecstasy in His Natural Immanence.

Q: The young rebels of the 1930s found their means of striking back at an objectionable society through political action. Today's generation seems disinclined to take any action at all. How do they hope to improve things if they don't take action, and if they don't take action can't they rightly be accused of irresponsibility and futilitarianism?
A: The political apathy of the Beat Generation is in itself a "political" movement; i.e., will influence political decisions in the future and possibly transfer politics to their rightful aims, i.e., sense.

"So long as he governs his people by the principle of nonassertion things naturally arrange themselves into social order." For, ". . . when a country is in confusion and discord, ideals of loyalty and patriotism arise" (Tao).

Q: What do you think have been the main achievements of the so-called "beat" writers, and what do you think their influence is or may be on younger writers?
A: Neal Cassady, although never published, wrote the greatest piece of the Beat Generation, a 40,000 word letter addressed to me in New York in 1950, which was the greatest story ever read by any American writer in American history.

Gregory Corso is a gigantic poet ("Gasoline" is only a hint). William Seward Burroughs is the secret shadow hovering over world literature. Al Ginsberg is, of course, a poet's poet. Gary Snyder and Philip Whalen are the magicians of West Coast poetry. (Kenneth) Rexroth appeals to me as a poet of great grandeur, I don't care if he doesn't like me. Mike McClure is wild. Naturally the younger kids will pick up from them.

Q: To some it appears that the days of the beat generation in San Francisco are numbered. You've gone to Long Island, Ginsberg and Corso to Europe, Snyder to Japan, Whalen to the East Bay. How do you view what seems to be the end of the literary beats here?
A: Originally I came from New England and Long Island anyway. San Francisco was my mad, wild playtown. Ginsberg's home is in Patterson,

Corso's in Manhattan. Snyder was actually born in S. F. Whalen is Oregonian. The literate beats will make it just the same (there are some hidden geniuses in S. F. yet to speak), and of course you have your Rexroth and (Lawrence) Ferlinghetti and Robert Stock and Ronny Loewinsohn and others.

When Stan Persky of Chicago hits S. F. you will have your new poet. Who cares about geography? But yes, San Francisco is the poetry center of America today.

St. Jack (Annotated by Jack Kerouac)
Al Aronowitz / 1959

From Al Aronowitz, *The Blacklisted Masterpieces of Al Aronowitz* (Bearsville, N.Y.: The Author, 1981). Reprinted with permission.

He was dressed in one of those heavy, flannel work shirts, tails hanging loose, that he always seems to wear on the jackets of his books and that makes it seem as if only his books have jackets. He was dressed in baggy pants and old shoes and his hair, uncombed and black, was blowing in the silent February sunlight. He looked as if he had just stepped out of one of his novels, or was about to step back into one, picking cotton, perhaps, in a California field next to his girl friend, of Mexican amber, and her little son, who picked cotton faster than he could as he cut his fingertips trying to earn a day's food for the three of them and a night's love for the two, a love that had brought him to a life only a poor Mexican could know and that was both as fierce and tender as all his other loves and as restless and as short.[1] Or maybe rushing in clunker shoes,[2] he calls them, to catch his train as a brakeman on the Southern Pacific, running like the football star he once had been,[3] or maybe just to catch it as a hobo going nowhere, seemingly, but always, really, going someplace, riding in a box car or an open gondola in summer heat or bitter cold, catching the cold, sometimes, but never the bitterness. Or perhaps smoking marijuana, in the same clothes, at a Denver society party, confounding the society at the party with a drunkenness that is so much less sophisticated than the liquored drunkenness of themselves but so much more knowing, or perhaps smoking it in a brothel on the way to Mexico City,

1. "I put 'cut fingertips' instead of 'mincing' to describe the effect of inexperiencedly picking cotton (also, 'mincing' sounds funny, like I was a fairy)"; Jack Kerouac to AGA, Jan 12, 1960.

2. "My shoes were 'clunkers,' not clunkety-clunk, in 'Railroad Earth'"; Jack Kerouac to AGA, January 12, 1960.

3. "I put in proper 'was' for football star, as clippings [enclosed with this letter—ed.] prove, and please, Al, send the clippings back (one sports reporter on *Newsday*, Stan Isaacs, doesn't believe I was a football star, and others too, like I suppose people wouldn't believe that Herman Melville was a whalingman)"; Jack Kerouac to AGA, January 12, 1960.

the smoke of it turning the brothel from a place of crawling flesh to a place of fleshy enchantment. Or maybe sitting as a forest ranger, alone for two months on a desolation mountain peak called Desolation, shouting Frank Sinatra songs at the stars above or the canyons below, and hearing the canyons and even the stars answer him.[4] Or perhaps racing from one of these places to the other, from the East Side to the West Coast, sometimes in ninety-mile-an-hour cars, sometimes in slower buses, and once on the back of an Okie's truck, standing with other hitchhikers, laughing, urinating into the wind, and he says woe unto those who spit on the Beat Generation, the wind'll blow it back. He was on the road in front of his house, not so symbolic as other roads he had traveled, perhaps, but certainly as unpaved, and he walked through the mud carrying a shopping bag a head taller than himself.

"Beer," said Jack Kerouac. "Refreshments for the afternoon. Come on in."

He pointed the way with a quick toss of the chin that sent his hair flying into a new state of disorder, and he walked toward a rear kitchen door, staggering, somewhat prematurely, under his load. At the door was his mother, smiling and cheerful in an unexpected cliché, with eyeglasses, an apron, long, woolen stockings and a housewife's bandana tied around her head.

"Dorothy Kilgallen wrote in her column that I live in a thirty-thousand dollar mansion on Long Island," he said, his voice, like his face, youthful and tenor and full of strange, friendly gusto. "Does this look like a thirty-thousand-dollar mansion? If I paid thirty thousand dollars for it, I sure got cheated, huh? I only paid fourteen," and for the word fourteen, he dropped his voice, like the price of the house, to a near-baritone, making the fourteen sound even lower and even mysterious.

The house was like many other older generation houses in Northport,[5] members of the Weatherbeaten Generation, perhaps. It was large and

---

4. "Various inserts . . . singing to Frank Sinatra, 'up the stars,' etc., are obvious, and you should put them in for accuracy and tone of article"; Jack Kerouac to AGA, January 12, 1960.

5. Kerouac cut the word "Northport" and changed it to "Long Island." "Yes, Sterling [Lord, Kerouac's agent] and I do not want mention of Northport; you said that 'it should be left in the record that I once lived there.' I STILL live there; I do not want carloads of zen beatnik hipsters scouting my yard and house? How'd you expect me to get work done here? Have you no idea of the number of people who would like to 'meet' me and visit me? Don't you know it runs in the thousands and thousands, mostly teenagers full of insane desire to be big Dean Moriarty's? And all kinds of people, even recently some of Carl Solomon's [friend of Kerouac and Ginsberg, to whom *Howl* was dedicated] friends from the nut-house got on my milk route and what can you really expect from them? My mother is old and quiet and needs her quietness at home. Well, now you understand"; Jack Kerouac to AGA, undated.

wooden with porches, front and rear, and a sag but no swing. It was surrounded by trees, hedges and other surviving marks of rusticity and it was covered by a recent, but unsuccessful, coat of camouflage, battleship gray.

"This isn't even our furniture," said his mother, a short, not yet rotund woman of sixty-four, who spoke with that distinct but almost indefinable accent that the French-Canadians have. "This furniture came with the house. They're always printing things about Jack that aren't true—you know, about the Beat Generation and all that juvenile delinquency. Everybody says, 'Beat Generation!—He's a juvenile delinquent!' But he's a good boy—a good son. He was never any juvenile delinquent. I know, I'm his mother."

"Yeah," he added. "We're middle class, we've always been middle class. We're middle class just like you," and he offered to conduct a sight-seeing tour through the house. The furniture clearly was middle class, with overtones of mahogany and over-stuffing of couches and if it hadn't been theirs to begin with, it certainly seemed to have come from the past he wrote about in *Dr. Sax*, his childhood and his adolescence in the big tenement flats of Lowell, Massachusetts, where, son of a printer who was also a pool hall and bowling alley operator, he played with marbles, traded comic books, imitated the Shadow, and didn't miss any of the most important films of the thirties, not realizing until long afterwards that what he laughed at in Harpo Marx delight was really Kafkaesque commentary on contemporary civilization.

"We got the house through an agent, a real estate agent," he said. "We saw an ad in the *New York Times*, and we bought it," and he pronounced the ought in bought somewhere between ought and ott, a legacy, too, of Lowell, although other aspects of his speech, his animation, his accents, his undulating rhythms, were strangely far western. "We bought it from the Eddys—George Eddy and Mona Kent Eddy, you must have heard of her. She wrote the radio serial—*Portia Faces Life*. She's very famous," and there was a factualness to his very famous that sounded as if it had come from two thousand quarter-hours of listening. "She paints, too. She gave me that picture for Christmas."

He walked toward a small framed canvas above the server in the dining room, with its early American chairs and tables and all looked down upon by a modern plastic bubble lamp that hung from the ceiling, and he surveyed the painting for a moment, commenting, "Look at that, ehh?" Then he turned back and continued walking through the house, saying: "Everybody thinks I've got a couple of my books published I'm a millionaire. I've only made, maybe twenty thousand dollars, and bought this house. And all those years, and didn't get anything published, and now all of a sudden I'm supposed to be a millionaire. But nobody says anything about those eight years I didn't make any money at all, except what I made when I was working on the railroad."

In the kitchen, his mother, with an affability that apparently had endured for years, was unpacking the contents of the shopping bag, transferring the cans of beer into one of the many cabinets beneath the long counter tops that had never been imagined when the house was built. Quickly, he salvaged what he could from the bag, filling both hands. "I owe everything to her. Come on upstairs. We'll have some beer and talk."

"You go ahead," his mother said. "If I watch television, will that interrupt you?" and she sat down in the parlor to the still unexorcised thrills of an afternoon quiz show.

"I watch television," he said, leading the way up the front step. "*San Francisco Beat*—you know that television show with the two big cops. Two big plainclothes cops running around grabbing these bearded beatniks. On television, yeah. And the bearded beatniks always have guns and they're beatin' the cops." He chuckled and, still chuckling, added: "I never knew beatniks had guns. And I saw Truman Capote. He said"—and he mimicked in a high-pitched voice, easy for him—"he said, 'Oh, they don't write, they typewrite.'"

He entered an upstairs bedroom that, with a desk, a typewriter, a tape recorder, books, papers, all in neat piles on the upstairs bedroom furniture, had been turned into a study. It overlooked the road.

"I don't sleep here," he said, motioning toward the bed. "I sleep in another room with the windows wide open, winter and summer. We have plenty of rooms, so we use them all. I like to sleep late sometimes . . . Don't get up till noon, one o'clock . . . I never thought I'd make money writing, either . . . Initially, art is a duty.[6] It's an old theory of mine in teenage notebooks and was culled from Dostoyevsky's holy diary. In other words, when I wrote these books, I did it as a 'holy duty' and thought my manuscripts would be discovered after I was dead, never dreamed they'd make money . . ."

He offered a can of beer, punched one open for himself, took a long swallow, sat back in a chair at the desk and suddenly became engrossed in a rush of thoughts, phrases, ideas, the poetry of his brain, mouthing some of it

6. The last two sentences of that paragraph are an insert by Kerouac; Jack Kerouac to AGA, January 12, 1960.

silently to himself, his lips moving, mumbling, as he looked out the window, alone, to himself, in the room, and in his pocket a notebook and a pencil, always there, ready to catch these droppings of his mind, but he didn't take them out of his pocket, he returned to the conversation. It was about one of those nights in 1957, a year before, when he had been reading his poetry in a cellar night club, the Village Vanguard, and the newspapers, with the verbal sneers that are journalese for satire, had laughed at him. He walked over to a dresser near the bed and pulled open a drawer. The dresser turned out, like the whole bedroom, to be nothing but a front for his literary activities. Inside there were none of the bed-clothes or underclothes or other garments that might be expected in a dresser drawer but rather several piles of manuscripts, all of them quite naked, and an old, thick scrapbook, which although not quite naked, too, was losing its covers. He pulled out he scrapbook and began leafing through its pages, stopping several times but only momentarily. On one page there was a clipping from the *New York Times* of November 18, 1939 . . .

> Point-starved by Tome for two straight years, Horace Mann's football squad yesterday shook off the jinx personified by the Maryland team, as Jack Kerouac a shifty, flat-footed back from Lowell, Mass., and the spearhead of the Maroon and White attack made a touchdown dash . . .

On another page, there was a clipping from another New York newspaper, unidentified . . .

> . . . Lou Little is basking away up at Cape Cod and dreaming about those long runs from reverse that Jack Kerouac, sophomore wingback, is going to gear off for the grid Lions next fall . . .

He continued leafing and now there was something of an incongruity between the clippings at the front and the clippings at the back, the incongruity of sports reviews and book reviews. He opened the scrapbook, finally, to a page which contained an article about him reading at the Village Vanguard.

"Oh, it was all right," he said. "But I guess I was feeling morbid . . . drunk . . ." and his voice suddenly took on that mood. "I just can't take this kind of stuff anymore"—and now, without a pause, his voice brightened with a bright idea—"I'm going to move to Florida. I'm going to get a house in the

country . . . In the country near my sister's . . . Oh, about ten miles out. I'm
too close to New York here. I get telegrams . . . I'm supposed to call *Life* today.
I'm sick of dealing with brainwashed journalists who think that facetiousness
is funny or that bad news better be better than good news or they'll lose their
jobs. They build their own Hells.[7]

"That time at the Vanguard? I was drunk on pernod. That was a Sunday
afternoon. They made me read something over again that I didn't want to
repeat. I also read a thing where I had to sing from *On the Road* . . . What was
horrible about that afternoon, what really upset me, you know, I had an old
prep school buddy from Horace Mann, Dick Sheresky who owns restaurants
around New York—you know Sheresky? Hadn't seen him for millions of years
and he comes up to me and instead of saying 'Dick—there you are!' I was so
decadent by this time with all these cops coming in back and saying I had to
join the police union or something—police card—and big gangsters coming
in or something to make me join the union, and kids pulling at my sleeves,
I say"–and his voice assumed a whining wise guy's voice in an imitation of
himself—"I say, 'ah Dick the Schmick,' I said to Dick. He said 'That's a good
one.' He was the wit at school, he was the funniest guy. He bought me a pernod. But I wasn't polite to him or his friend. His friend turned to me and
said, 'Do you think that *On the Road* is a joke?' I said"—and the disgust in his
voice now seemed as much as disgust with himself as with the question—
"I said, 'Ahhh, everything's a joke!' and I walked away . . .

"Was I a Buddhist then? Well, I couldn't be, a Buddhist has got to be
alone." He laughed at the thought. "A night club Buddhist!" Then he reflected
for a moment. "Ahhh, I was a Buddhist, yeah . . ."

He had also read that afternoon at the Village Vanguard a selection from the
Evergreen Review, one of his stories called "October in the Railroad Earth."

"I can write like that," he said with a quick and sure enthusiasm. "In fact,
I have a nice method for that. That's spontaneous writing. Spontaneous and
before breakfast in the morning. That's when you're real fresh. You got to
have a good typewriter. I could hardly sleep when I wrote that. I could hardly
talk. One Friday. Fifty-three. That part in the *Evergreen Review*, that's only
half of it. I have the other half of it untyped—I have to retype it double

---

7. "A long insert about what I think about *Life Magazine*, etc. 'Brainwashed journalists who build
their own hells.' If you don't put these things in I'll know your article on the Beat Gen. was a hatchet-
job ordered by Wechsler. . . . but this volume is not for the *Post*, it's for posterity"; Jack Kerouac to
AGA, January 12, 1960.

spaced for the publishers." He laughed to himself again. "Ol' Truman Capote. He said—and once more he mimicked—'It isn't writing, it's typewriting.' But it's hard to do it fast, spontaneous . . . You don't do it sentence by sentence. Sentences are stumbling blocks to language! Who in the hell started this sentence business? Like, John Holmes, I've watched him write. He writes on a typewriter so fast, but he gets stumped—he can't think of the proper word. I don't do that. If I can't think of the proper word, I just do bdlbdlbdlbdlbdlbdlbdl. Or else, bdlbdlbluuuuuuh. Right now, I'm typing up another one of my novels . . ." and he pointed into the drawer again toward the largest mass of manuscript . . . "*Visions of Neal*—Neal Cassady . . . he's a friend of mine in California. *On the Road* was all about him. He's a brakeman on the Southern Pacific . . . *Visions of Neal*, that's a huge one—that's this one here. We're going to publish thirty-eight pieces of it. Seven dollars and a half. Limited edition. You see, in my serious writing, I'm Jack through it all. But everybody else, their names are changed. I always had the same names, but the editors changed them, the publishers changed them. Ray Smith is Jack, Sal Paradise is Jack, Leo Percepied is Jack . . ."

His mother smiled through the doorway.

"Am I disturbing you?" she asked.

"No!" he answered. "No! Come on in and say something."

"What should I say?" she asked, "What should I tell you? I have two children. A daughter. She's married and she lives in Florida. And Jack. He's not married. I had another son, older than him, but he died. Gerard."

"I was four," Jack said. "He was nine. That's another book I wrote. *Visions of Gerard*. In *On the Road* I wrote I had a brother, but that was really my brother-in-law. When you're writing true stories about the world you simply have to throw everybody off for the sake of the law. The rest is fiction, idle daydreams."

"There's a lot of things he wrote in *On the Road*," his mother said, "that really don't belong in there."

"No," he insisted. "It's all true. Neal knows it's true. Only the names are changed."

"Well," his mother said, "I'll tell you right now, he's always lived with me, outside of when he travels. He wanted to write a book, to write something different, so he asked me and he took off one day and he did. So, anyhow, after they read the book, they write an awful lot of things about him that's not so—I know, I'm his mother. He lives with me all his life. Once in a while, he takes off, he goes on a trip, he sails away to Spain, he visits all his friends, you know, for a few months, but he comes back, he always has his home with me—unless he gets married and goes away someplace. But as long as he wants to live with me, it's all right. But when he did travel, I was working, you know, while he was away. I was making good money, he never wanted for anything. He would say where to send it, and there was always money there, I used to send it any time he needed it, for food, shoes, clothes—I was working . . ."

"She was working in a shoe factory," he said.

". . . Oh, I was making good money," she continued. "We're middle class—we've always been that way . . ."

"We're bourgeois," he said.

". . . We never had luxuries or many elaborate things," she added, "but we always had a good home, plenty to eat—"

"Sunday roasts!" Jack interrupted.

"—New clothes to wear," she continued. "He don't wear it, but it's true. We're just like any other ordinary people, working people, go to shows once in a while, travel a little bit. As far as I know of him, he's never been a delinquent or anything. You know, because he travels around a lot, that doesn't mean anything, he's really a nice boy. And kind. He's kind to everybody . . ."

"I used to be, anyway," he interrupted again.

". . . And that's all I can say," she concluded. "He never had a beard in his life, although I think he'd be better off myself if he had one."

"Yeah," he said. "Clifton Fadiman had on TV—a guy with a beard on a motorcycle with a portable typewriter typing as he rode along."

"Two years ago, he took me to California," she said, "and he took me all around—"

"I took her to Berkeley," he said. "I used to live in Berkeley."

"And I met some of those fellows there," she said. "They didn't look bad to me—none of them acted really bad, and one of them, Philip Whalen, he was very nice.[8] Well, they were polite. You know, when he wrote this book, *Town and the City*, he used to dress up like a bank robber . . ."

"I didn't make any money on *The Town and the City*," he said. "Just two, three thousand dollars."

"Oh, more than that," she said, "Four, anyhow. When you went to Denver."

8. "When my mother said she liked 'one of them' in Calif. she meant Whalen"; Jack Kerouac to AGA, January 12, 1960.

"You know, I spent three years writing *Town and the City*," he said. "I spent twenty-one days writing *On the Road*. *Town and the City*, that was my first book, that was a novel-type novel. It had characters and development and all that. It was mostly fiction. Fiction is nothing but idle day dreams. Look what I did with *Town and the City*—I gave my father a nice big house, I gave my mother three daughters to help her wash the dishes, I gave myself four brothers to keep me company, protect me. Baaaaah! Idle day dreams! The way to write is with real things and real people. How else are you going to have the truth!"

"When he was writing *Town and the City*," his mother said, "my husband was very sick at the time and I had to work to support the house. So he stayed home and took care of his father. He could handle his father—I couldn't. You know, he had to carry him around and take him to the bathroom and clean him and all that and the things I couldn't do. And I was making enough money to support everybody because I had a good job."

"I was writing a chapter when he died," Jack said, "and I thought he was snoring in the next room, you know, a loud snore—"

"It was not a snore," she interrupted, "it was a . . ."

"Death rattle," he said. "But I was typing away, and so I missed out on it. And you know, that . . . that was terrible. I went around to go see him because he had stopped snoring, and I thought he was sleeping . . ."

"He was fifty-five." she said.

"Fifty-seven." he corrected.

"Honest?" she said. "I thought he was fifty-five."

"Cancer of the spleen," he said.

There was the quiet of sadness unwillingly remembered, of thoughts buried in the mind ten years before, but the mind is a shallow grave.

"Well, anyhow," his mother said, "I want to show you something. It's very simple. It'll only take a minute."

She walked six steps out the door and through the upstairs hall into her son's open window bedroom. "If he was so bad," she said, pointing toward a silver crucifix over the headboard, "would he have that? And that?"—and she pointed to a string of rosary beads on his night table—"He wore that around his neck, but they broke. They were blessed by Trappist monks."

Jack stood watching, holding his beer can, his second or his third, something like a sponsor, perhaps, listening to a commercial and then he pointed, beneath the crucifix, showing off with the same pleasure that it gave him, a night-light with a pull chain attached to the headboard and a sheaf of notepaper in a clipboard hanging from the adjacent wall.

"I just fixed this up," he said, pulling the string to light the bulb and taking the clipboard from its hook, from which also dangled a pencil, "I use them to write down dream thoughts. I hear them in a dream and wake up and turn the light on and write them down. You know, like Old Angel Midnight."

He read what was written on the top sheet, the previous night's message "Go, tell the ash with the fish, all he needs is illuminating . . . Man's will, which is already recorded in heaven—strange will . . . Death makes a stand in its own darkness. I can get more grace from a snot nose wart brain . . ."

"These are what I call bedside sheets," he said, "you know, sheets hanging by the bedside."

"Who ever heard of anything—is that what you have hanging in the window there?" his mother asked. "Is that where you got the idea?"

"Huh?" he said.

"Those are bed sheets Mrs. Eddy put up—" she said.

"No," he corrected, "bedside sheets, pieces of paper hanging by the bedside!"

"Oh," she said, "explain yourself."

"I did," he chuckled. "You don't listen. You're airing sheets."

He walked back into his study and, looking at the clipboard, read again, this time slowly, so it could be copied: "Man's will, comma, which is already recorded in heaven . . . dash . . ." and then he added, almost as if it were an after thought, "strange will!" saying strange will as if it were a whistle of amazement, whew-whew! "period . . ." and liking the sound of it, he repeated "strange will!" again in tune to whew-whew! but this time more softly, "Death makes a stand in its own darkness"—and he chuckled again, and, still chuckling, continued—"I can get more grace from a snot nose wart brain"—

"Oh, God!" his mother said.

"I can get more grace from a snot nose wart brain," he repeated, chuckling all the way through, "—I can tell I was doubtful with that!"

"Who understands these things?" his mother said. "I don't."

"Well," he said, "it means I'm mad, I'm not getting enough grace, I can get more grace from a snot nose wart brain than I can from heaven . . ."

"Well, what's that mean?" she said.

"It's just a religious thought," he said, and he chanted to himself: " 'Snot . . . nose . . . wart . . . brain . . .' Those are dream thoughts. I hear them in a dream and I wake up."

"You're worse than I am," she said. "When I dream about something, it's always cute."

He swallowed some beer, and, voiceless, began forming phrases with his mouth again, more thoughts, dream thoughts perhaps in the middle of the day. He looked out the window, his eyes on the road, his face as abstract as what was behind it. It was a visitation, if not of Old Angel Midnight or of Old Angel Daylight, then certainly of the Muse. But then, he seemed to have many angels and, judging by the number of drawers in the dresser and by what they contained, he seemed to have many visitations. He mumbled, with a sound intelligible only to himself, several phrases of this private imagery, which, once written, would be intelligible to so many others—others who, in the coffee shops of New York's Greenwich Village, in the bars of San Francisco's North Beach, even now had beatified him, calling him, with the same spontaneity of his typewriter, St. Jack.

"Oh, sure," he said, returning to the conversation, "they're going to write lots of books about me . . . After I'm dead? Like Hemingway . . . Criticisms . . . they have some about Hemingway already . . . Biographies. I mean before he dies? . . . I'm kind of sensitive."—and there was a conveyed embarrassment in his sensitive—"I used to be a naive, overbelieving type."

"I haven't read all his books," his mother said. "He told me one time that if I read the book, *On the Road*, I'd get mad at him, so I read up to page thirty-four—I quit. I didn't get mad at him that far back, but I will read it some day when I quiet down."

"She can read *The Dharma Bums*," he said, "That's nice. But I told her not to read *The Subterraneans* at all . . . My sister read it. She likes everything I do, my sister."

"She's a cute girl," his mother said, "wonderful girl. She's not at all like he is. Day and Night!"

"She's a bookkeeper," he said, and he took another drink of beer. "*The Dharma Bums*," I wrote that after *On the Road* came out. I said to Viking, 'I'll get you another book.' And Malcom Cowley, my editor, said 'Please write another book like *On the Road*" with adventures about people. Stop talking about yourself.' It's got good sentences, *Dharma Bums*. I spent five hundred dollars having it restored to my original way I wrote it. They . . . they took *Dharma Bums* and changed it—made three thousand commas and stuff, type changes, rearrangements, sentence rearrangements. I rearranged everything back to the way I wrote it . . . and got a bill for five hundred dollars. The bill said 'alterations.' But what it is restorations! The way they fixed it was awful. They said 'That's our house style here at Viking' and he said it sweetly, " 'That's our house style here at Viking.' Did you ever hear of a house style?—Well, that's all right for newspapers, or whore houses, but not publishers. *On the Road* sold twenty thousand hard cover copies. And now, five hundred thousand soft covers are being sold . . ."

"Paper backs, they're called." his mother said.

"Paper backs, yeah," he said. "Five hundred thousand. A penny a copy for me. But we sold *Dharma Bums* to soft cover people for ten thousand. I get five. *On the Road* and *Dharma Bums* are almost even, I think now. *The Subterraneans* made more money than the others because MGM took it—fifteen grand! . . . I should have settled for ten times that much . . ."

"You know," his mother said, "when you look in the papers and read about these fellows that the movie people take their books, one hundred thousand . . ."

"A hundred and sixty-five!" he said, his voice in imitation of a headline. "I don't know anything about business . . . But it was a beginning. *The Subterraneans* is all over the world—Japan, Argentina, everybody's taking it"—and there was a surprise in his voice, which he quelled with another beer. "I had sold the movie rights to *On the Road*, too, but then they reneged. Two thousand option money. Yeah, that was Mort Sahl and Joyce Jamison and a bunch of guys. They should have taken it . . . it's a good production. Now, nobody has it. Jerry Wald keeps writing a letter every six months, saying 'I'm thinking about it–it's a tough plot.' Everybody thinks it's sold, so they don't ask for it. In fact, I thought of making an ad in Billboard—'ON THE ROAD—NOT SOLD!' Then if I got a big chunk of money, you know what I'd do with it? Five percent in something, five percent, you know, check every month. That'd be nice. Then I could, you know, bring fellows to India and all that stuff, go out and do things, and all that money's free, see? And you'd have your check," he said, turning toward his mother.

"Well, I'm going downstairs now," she said, "and I'll make you some little sandwiches, they're not meat but I think you'll like them . . ."

"Well, finish your story," he said.

"Which story?" she said. "I haven't got much of a story to tell, outside that I was your benefactor all my life," and she laughed. "I'm sixty-three now, I'm going to be sixty-four next week . . ."

"And we're going to go to Radio City," he said.

"...Time flies!" she said. "God! The years go by so fast after sixty. But I don't care. If I keep healthy, that's the main thing. I got fat now, you know, I wasn't always this fat. But I stopped wearing girdles, you know, and I'm spreading..."

"You know, her favorite is Genevieve there on television," he said, then repeating, with a half-French pronunciation: "Genevieve. How do you spell her name?"

"Genevieve," she said. "It's G-E-N-E-V-I-E-V-E."

"Well, that's pronounced Gen-e-vieve, isn't it?" he said.

"In French, let me tell you," she said, "in French, JAN-VIEVE! JAN! JAN-VIEVE!"

"Say something in French," he said.

"Qu'est-ce-que tu veux savoir?" she said.

"She tutoied you," he said, and then he added, turning toward her and correcting her: "Tu tutoye. Qu'est-ce-que VOUS voulez savoir?"

There was a pride in her French as well as a difference. It was the pride of a French which the French-Canadians believe is a preservation of the language of France before Louis XIV, when German and Moorish influences began to shape it to it's present sounds. It was the language which the emigres had brought to Canada with them, just as they had brought the name Kerouac.[9] Now, of course, the name was returning to France on book covers. And when G. Claude Gallimard, the French publisher, had visited America some months before, he had said: "I must meet him. I must meet your Jacques Kerouac." And so Barney Rosset, the head of Grove Press, had arranged a dinner at his home.

"That afternoon there," he said, reminding his mother, "when the Filipino butler..."

"Oh, yeah," his mother said, "oh, my goodness! They gave me a couple of drinks and they made them so strong. I don't know what happened."

9. "In the French-talking part, where I say 'tu tutoye' you don't use an accent egue over the 'e' in 'tutoye' (present tense).... And in French the name is Kerouac with the accent egue. And Michel Mohrt did say the French my mother and I spoke was pure eighteenth century Norman French, which was substantiated recently by visiting Quebecois scholar here at the house. In other words, 'French-Canadian' is a pure preservation of old pre-Louis XIV French before the influence of Moorish and Germanic on the French language which has now resulted in 'Parisia' guttural that you hear in French movies (however NOT in Jean Gavin and Maurice Chevalier, by the way, who are Normans). This is facts. Do you realize that everybody in Quebec is delighted with the French in *Doctor Sax*?"; Jack Kerouac to AGA, January 12, 1960.

"We talked French," he said. "We had a big, screaming dinner, all talking French. Don Allen and Barney Rosset—you know, from Grove Press—they were quiet. They didn't know what to say. Michel Mohrt announced I was speaking pure eighteenth century Norman French."

"It was delicious, though," she said. "We had a wonderful dinner. I was all over the place. I had to leave the men by themselves, you know. And I played the piano, though I don't play very good, and then I went downstairs and I kidded with the butler, the little butler . . ."

"Then we started," he said, "then my mother and I started roaming up the street, hitting all the bars, Fifth Avenue, Schmifth Avenue . . . And then I was supposed to go to *Holiday Magazine* to meet an interviewer and we got there late . . ."

"I'll never do that again," his mother said. "Well, I had just come back from Florida, and we had settled down here, and I hadn't been to New York in quite a while, and we were having a ball out there, and . . . I overstepped my line," and she laughed. "Oh, I had too much, might as well come out with it, I had too much to drink, although I should at my age, you know, be careful. But I was having a big time. I was with him . . . Yeah, he drinks a little, I think a little too much for his own health, his own good health.

"Yeah," he said, "If I was away from home, I'd drink too much. I don't drink much here."

"In Florida, when we lived there," she said, "he didn't drink at all, only sometimes on weekends he would go and get a little bottle if we had company—my son-in-law would come, you know. We had beer and wine. But over here, there's always somebody coming in and out and he's been to parties around here, and, oh, my! One drink after another!"

"I wanted to come here and hide out, you know," he said, "and the guy that owns this house insists on having me meet everybody—George Eddy, you know, like Nelson Eddy. Mona Kent Eddy's husband . . ."

"I like them," his mother said, "but all their friends they want me to meet! Jack's friends, there's one I can't stand. That's right. Allen Ginsberg. Because there's something about that man I just can't stand. And I'm afraid of him. And then one time, I read a letter he sent to Jack, and he was insulting a priest, a Catholic priest that had befriended him . . ."

"He was telling Franciscan monks," Jack said, "to take their clothes off. In Italy, on a lawn outside the monastery in Assisi."

"That burned me up," she said. "And then my husband couldn't stand him, either. And when my husband died"—

"He's one of my closest friends," Jack said. "She doesn't like my girl friend, either."

"And before my husband died," she continued, "he made me promise, never to let . . . to try to keep Allen Ginsberg out of the house. It's the only one he didn't like . . ."

"She likes Neal Cassady." Jack said.

"Neal's all right," his mother said. "He is all right. No fooling. He's a little eccentric and he loves to play the horses—that's what makes him so nervous, I guess. He used to come to our house in Richmond Hill, and that fellow couldn't stay put on the chair more than a second. He would jump from one place to another. He was always active. I never met his wife and children, though I'm told they're very nice."

Jack's mother rose off her seat on the edge of the bed and suddenly hurried from the room.

"I got a letter from Henry Miller, two or three days ago," Jack announced. "See what it says here? He says," and he turned about, picked up a sheet of paper from his desk top and began reading in a rapid, chirping style: " 'Dear Jack, Right-o for all your ills, laughter. So said the master, Rabelais. Northport sounds even more remote than Big Sur' "—and he interpolated, "That's not true." Then he continued reading: " 'But no matter where you are now, you'll be pestered. I don't worry about you. You're tough, resilient, gay and suicidal in a healthy way. Carry on! Allez-y! Au bout du monde, Baudelaire et cetera.' He says, 'One day, I'll just quit, probably with pen in hand. All the best now. Du courage, quoi! Henry.' See, he's going to write the preface for the soft cover edition of *The Subterraneans*."[10]

In a moment, his mother had returned, carrying a book that was leather-bound.

"This is *The Town and the City*," she said. "This is the first book that he ever came out with. Read what it says there. That tells the whole story," and she opened the book to its inside cover and a message, written in ink: To my dear mother, Gabe—

10. "Don't say that I read Henry Miller all my life, it just isn't true, I did read Louis Ferdinand Celine, from whom Miller obtained his style. I never could find a copy of the Tropics anyway. I think Miller is a great man but Celine, his master, is a giant"; Jack Kerouac to AGA, January 12, 1960. Miller did not, as it turned out, write the introduction to *The Subterraneans*.

"That's for Gabrielle," she said. "That's my name."

—From your loving son, your humble son. No mother could have given stronger support over the harsh years to her son, without which no book would have been written at all. And no mother in this world was ever so wise, so good, so dear, and so sweet as you are. Here's hoping this book will help repay you at last for a life of toil, humility and true piety and gladden your heart, and Pa's, which will gladden mine. All my love, Jean.

"That's my real name." Jack said.
"Isn't that cute?" his mother asked, and she hurried out of the room again, returning seconds later with another book. "Here's a funny one. This is *The Dharma Bums*—look at that," and again she turned to an inscription inside the cover: To Ma, Timmy and Tyke—
"Aaaah," Jack said. "Timmy's gone. Got run over."
"The cat," his mother said.
"Two cats," he said.

—A third adventure to pay for the house, the cat food, the brandy and the peaceful sleep. From Dharma Bum Jack, Ti Jean. Mom, you're on pages one-thirty-two, one-thirty-three, one-forty-eight.

"Isn't that sweet," she said, laughing, and he laughed, too. Then she went for another book, also leather-bound.
"Here's another one," she said. "This is *On the Road*. That's a cute one."
"It's a special bound copy," Jack said. "They only make one."
"He gave it to me," she said, and she opened it, too, to the inscription.

To ma—This book, which will buy you the little cottage you always wanted where you'll find—

"It bought this house," Jack said, with another chuckle. "Just about paid cash for it. Gave them seven thousand and then six months later gave them another seven. That doesn't include the furniture . . ."
"Oh, no," his mother added. "They're going to come and get that stuff out of here."
"That's their chair," Jack said, motioning toward one.

"They took some furniture out and left some in," his mother said. "There's some more they have to take, like this mirror and the stuff downstairs . . ."

—complete peace and happiness for the first time in your long and helpful life. From Ti Jean, your son, the author. Jack Kerouac. January fourteenth, 1958.

"See, I get them all," his mother said. "Now I got to read them."

"She hasn't got *The Subterraneans*," Jack said, and then, after she had gone downstairs to prepare the sandwiches, he added: "You know, *The Subterraneans*, it's about a love affair with a Negro girl."

He leaned back with his beer can again, his fourth or fifth. "I can take it," he said. "You know, as I say, Li Po and all those other guys drank. Li Po, the Chinese poet,"—and chuckling: "I don't mean Edgar Allan! I remember James Wechsler—he said I didn't believe in peace. Awww, he's a politician. As Allen Ginsberg says, I'd hate to be a poet in a country where Wechsler is the Commissar of Poetry.[11] I'm not interested in politics. I'm interested in Li Po. He was a Dharma Bum type. You know, a poor poet, roaming China. You know, I have some eighteen-year-old writings that are pure Buddhism. I'm thirty-seven now. My birthday's March 12. So I've always been a Buddhist. When I was a little kid, I used to lock myself in the toilet whenever company would come. Once they couldn't open the door—I was locked in. But all this angry hipster stuff, it's all just an overjoyed bit of life . . . you know what this is like? It's like *Citizen Kane*. Remember the guy in *Citizen Kane* going around, getting all this, seeing old Joseph Cotten at the hospital. That's me. Then he goes to see the old Jewish publisher, remember that? Everett Sloane. There was a guy going around—who was it? You know when I saw it? I saw it Pearl Harbor day. I came out of the theater and saw the headlines about Pearl Harbor. It was a Sunday night . . ."

There were lines on his face now that darkened it, no more the picture of handsome beauty that once had adorned a page of *Mademoiselle* magazine but the reflection of his own verbal images, with his voice constantly playing the different roles, imitating the tones of others and himself, sometimes light, sometimes broody—broody now, but even in its broodiness, still mellow.

"I was in the Navy in World War II," he said. "A few months—six months. I was discharged. Schizoid personality," and he chuckled. "They gave me a

11. "Allen Ginsberg did say 'I'd hate to be a poet in a country where Wechsler is the Commissar of Poetry' so there's no harm in that insert, factually, and are you afraid of Wechsler? I'm not and never will be"; Jack Kerouac to AGA, January 12, 1960.

rifle and they had me marching out on the drill field, right turn, left turn, and I said, 'Awww, I don't want to do this,' and I dropped my rifle and I went into the library and I started to read. I told them, 'I don't want discipline and I'm not going to have discipline.' So they put me in the hospital. Then I went into the Merchant Marine. It was during the war, but I didn't get shot at. I mean, no torpedoes were fired at us. It was in 1940 I went to Columbia to play football. I played wingback. That's in the single wing, before the T—the guy who comes around, gets the reverse and comes waaay around the other end. I only played in my freshman year. I quit twice—quit the football team twice.

"See, I played football at Lowell High. Horace Mann High, for me it was a prep school to make up credits. To make up math and French. At Columbia, broke my leg in the game, third game of the year. I was out all the rest of the season with crutches, sitting in front of the fire in the Lion's Den, eating big steaks and hot fudge sundaes. It was great! And that's when I started reading Thomas Wolfe. I had the leisure, see, to read. I went back in the fall of '41 for the season. Now I was a sophomore and I was going to be on the varsity. And, I don't know, I was getting very poetic by that time, and I'd get black and broody and everything. Packed my suitcase and walked right out in front of Lou Little. He said, 'Where you going?' I said 'Oh, this suitcase is empty. I'm going to my grandmother's house to get some clothes.' I walked out with a full suitcase.

"Then I was a big poet and wanted to go down to Virginia and see the moon shining in Virginia. I went down to Virginia." And he laughed at himself. "Then I came back to work in filling stations and everything and went to sea, went to the North Pole, in the Merchant Marine. Got back in October 1942. And Lou Little—there was a telegram there saying, 'You can come back on the team if you want to take the bull by the horns.' I went back. Worked out a week, and the Army game came up—my great enemy, Henry Mazur, was making long runs for Army, captain of Army. Told Lou Little, 'Let me in there, man! I'm going to get him!' He's the guy in *The Town and the City* who pushed me out of the shower when I was a little kid. He played for Lowell High, too—he was a senior and I was a freshman. He was mean—I was going to get him in that game. And Lou didn't put me in that game, the Army game, so I said pooh"—and he pooh-spit—"and I quit.[12]

12. "I didn't 'spit' talking about Columbia football, I wouldn't spit on my mother's floor . . . I went 'Pooh!' . . . I 'pooh-spit' "; Jack Kerouac to AGA, January 12, 1960.

But the reason why I quit is deeper than that. I was just sitting in my room, and it was snowing, you know, the dorms, snow was falling, time to go to scrimmage, time to go out in the snow and the mud and bang yourself around. And on the radio, it started, you know—'Dum dum dum dummm-mmmmmm'—Beethoven!—'Dum dum dum dummmmmmmm'"—and he hummed the opening bars of Beethoven's Fifth Symphony. "I said," and now he whispered, "I said 'I'm going to be an artist! I'm not going to be a football player!' That's the night I didn't go to scrimmage. And I never went back to football, see?

"And shortly after, a month or so, I left the whole college. Because it was hard to keep going to an Ivy League school if you quit your football. They make it hard for you. The Ivy League is hypocritical, you know. Oh, I flunked in chemistry. I hate chemistry. Gee, I kept cutting it, I never went to class anyway. But I had an A in Shakespeare. With Mark Van Doren. And flunked chemistry. Well, after all that, yeah, I quit college and then back to sea. Got an apartment on the campus, the Columbia campus with my first wife before we were married. And all the students used to come in with books and bottles, hang around. My apartment was a hangout for the young intellectuals of the campus. My wife, her grandmother lived right there. Her grandmother lived right there. Her grandmother was an old friend of Nicholas Murray Butler's, and they lived in an old house next to Butler's. She was supposed to be living with her grandmother, but was living in sin with me in an apartment. And in walks Ginsberg, and in walks everybody else. Ginsberg, sixteen years old with his ears sticking out at that time. The first thing he said to me was, 'Discretion is the better part of valor'"—and he imitated Ginsberg with mock freshman earnestness, and then he laughed. "He was a freshman. But after a few years of that, Ginsberg really began to develop and became a hipster—whooooh!—the influence of Huncke. Herbert Huncke.

"Well, Ginsberg and I, there we are. And then there's this great figure we hear about, this great evil figure from St. Louis, Bill Burroughs. We go over, and he's just great! We sat at his feet and, well, Burroughs went around and found Huncke and found everybody else. We had a gang of friends from St. Louis. It was a St. Louis clique of rich guys from St. Louis, decadent intellectual types, fin de siecle, enfants terribles types, ugh! Allen and me? Well, we were poets together. I like the way he told long stories about New Jersey and everything. I've always had a friend like Allen. In Lowell, I had a friend,

Sebastian Sampas, who was just like him—you know, always a weird, poetic, Latin type. I always had a Latin friend somewhere who was a poet, somehow. Latin? Well, I mean dark, dark, mysterious, you know . . . Sebastian died on Anzio beachhead . . .

"But, you know, Allen and I got our start forming a circle around Burroughs and the guys from St. Louis—the whole thing really begins in St. Louis. And Harvard. Yeah, Burroughs went to Harvard. And Huncke's very important, you know, might be just as important as Neal, almost. He's the greatest story teller I ever met. I don't like his ideas about—a mugger and all that stuff. Of course, he doesn't do the mugging himself—he gets mugs to do it for him. He has a mug with him to do the mugging—he doesn't do it himself, he's just a little guy, you know. Bitter . . . or used to be, he's fine now . . . Allen and I started out among petty criminals, but we weren't criminals.[13] We were students in school—I was a seaman and he was a student. We were studying their personalities for poetic reasons, like Villon. We never did anything, except that Allen didn't know how to throw them out of the apartment. Yeah, he didn't know how to throw them out—they foisted themselves on him. And there was this big, tall, six-foot redhead there, Vicky. And she's the later Liz Martin in *The Town and the City*. The Liz Martin starts out as my little sister and grows up into a big evil Vicky. That wasn't a well-done book, but it was a great idea. The fascination was, as Norman Mailer would say, Hip. We had been to college, we had heard all that bull, and this was a new philosophy. And it found its most beautiful flower in Neal, who wasn't a petty criminal, you know, he wasn't a criminal. Yeah, a large natured man, much too much of a nature to be a criminal. Besides, Neal's a Jesuit. You know, he used to be a choir boy. Priests cried on his shoulder . . ."

Jack's mother bustled in with a trayfull of Friday sandwiches, tiny, tasty, prepared with housewife expertness and arranged in a display meant to be too pretty to eat but too appetizing not to. He asked her to get him another can of beer.

"I had two wives," he said. "Twenty-two years old I got married, and I got married again at twenty-eight. Each time the marriage lasted six months. The first wife was a rich girl from Michigan, and we didn't have any money

13. "Huncke was once bitter but isn't anymore . . . has sweetened completely"; Jack Kerouac to AGA, January 12, 1960.

or anything. We kept eating mayonnaise sandwiches. Well, 'Go back home
to your family and eat good!' Yeah, I was writing then. I was writing essays
on Yeats. Early novels, juvenile novels I have all over the place. She was
nice, and I actually sent her home because it would be better for her. But
the second—I didn't like her! She didn't like any of my friends, none of my
friends liked her. She was beautiful. I married her because she was beautiful . . .
Did they tell you about Bill Cannastra? The guy that jumped out of the
subway? He climbed out a subway window, said, 'We'll get one more beer at
the Remo.' Well, he had a loft. After he died, she moved into his loft. I met
her in the loft. I would wake up in the morning and look at her and how
beautiful she was. And then we would have to get out of bed and go to work.
She's remarried and has twins. She's alright, but she's always sending cops
after me. Sending cops after me for non-support. That's why I ran away to
California . . .

"My girl's name is Dody. She's a widow, she's the one that my mother
doesn't like. Because she has long, long hair, she doesn't tie it up. Because
she likes to go barefoot. Because she's an Indian. She's ninety-five percent
Indian. My mother calls her la sauvage—the savage. You know, she's a
very Bohemian painter, a very good painter. I just met her. All of us, you
know, the gang, just met her. They love her, too. Allen likes her. Everybody
loves her."

His mother brought him another can of beer and he punched a hole in it.

"Beat?" he said. "Yeah, I remember the scene. John Holmes and I
were playing jazz records and drinking beer allllll day on a gloomy"–and he
pronounced gloomy as if he were saying ugh!—"afternoon, and we were talking about the Lost Generation and 'What's this sad generation?' And we
thought of various names, and I say"—and he half whispered it—"I say, 'Ah,
this is really a Beat Generation!' And he leaped up and said, 'That's it! You've
got it!' See?" and Jack chuckled. "John says no? I remember, he forgot that. He
went 'Ahhhhh,' you know. He's a very nice kid, he's always enthusiastic. But
anyway, then I put it in the *On the Road* manuscript—the expression. But
he publicized 'Beat Generation' first before *On the Road* was published.
On the Road wasn't published for seven years. He publicized the expression
in the *New York Times*. And I got angry. Well, because the article he wrote
for the *New York Times* was a précis of the plot of *The Town and the City*.
And nobody seemed to want to believe that I made up the term, 'Beat
Generation.'

"I was going to use 'The Beat Generation' for the title of *On the Road*, but my editor, Malcolm Cowley, didn't want to. He said, 'Oh, *On the Road* is a better title.' That was my original title. Then I changed it to 'Beat Generation' and then back to *On the Road*. But I could write another novel and call it that—my next novel. I'm going to call it 'The Beat Generation' before I lose any, you know, lose out on that. I'd like to write a novel about getting published. You know, start off with me tramping along with a rucksack, all the way up to making a speech at Hunter College with James Wechsler, who accused me of not believing in peace.[14] Could end it there. And, you know, include all the cocktail parties, publishers' parties, wild weekends, TV appearances, nightclubs. That'd be a funny book, huh? Call it 'The Beat Generation' cause that's what they're all talking about. Now they're making a movie, now MGM's making a movie with that title, something about beatniks beating up housewives. But that's my title—they don't own that title! They didn't get it. We're going to sue 'em. My lawyer's going to sue 'em. My agent's lawyer. Sue 'em for the title . . .

"Allen . . . Allen said that Huncke said it first . . . 'Beat' . . . But Huncke didn't say 'Beat Generation.' He just said 'beat.' We learned the word from him. To me at first it meant being poor and sleeping in subways, like Huncke used to do, and yet being illuminated and having illuminated ideas about apocalypse and all that. It was quite different then. Then I went to Lowell, Massachusetts, in 1954. Got a room in Skid Row near the depot. Walked twenty miles around Lowell every day. Went to my old church where I got my first confirmation. Knelt, all alone, all alone in the church, in the great silence of the church . . . And I suddenly realized, beat means beatitude! Beatific! I was beatific in the church . . . See? It doesn't apply to anybody else, I don't think, the remembrance of your first vow."[15]

"What does it mean today? Beat Generation . . . Well, there was an article in the paper yesterday. A young kid with a beard. Said that Johnny Jones of East Islip, Long Island, over here, went to San Francisco to be a beatnik. Stayed there, lived in a cold water pad, he wrote poems and he hung around with

14. "I repeat that James Wechsler accused me of not believing in Peace, which is a terrible thing to say about anybody who is not a munitions maker"; Jack Kerouac to AGA, January 12, 1960.

15. "For 'beatific' paragraph I clarify about 'first confirmation' as my 'first vow—this is extremely important and clear . . . that's why it doesn't apply to 'anyone else' in the beat gen"; Jack Kerouac to AGA, January 12, 1960.

Negroes and jazz musicians. Finally he gave up in despair and called his mother long distance and cried and now he's coming home and shaving off his beard. You see, this is silly, it has nothing to do with the serious artists who started the whole thing just by, you know, writing the poem, writing the book. It's just a fad, just like the Lost Generation. I really think it's just a generation fad. *On the Road* was about what happened ten years ago. Today it's become famous and popular . . ."

He rose up from his chair with an invitation to follow him and walked into another bedroom, this one almost bare of furniture but with several large, recent canvases leaning against the wall and with a smaller one on an easel.

"I'm just starting to learn." he said, picking up a brush and dabbing at an indistinct brown figure against the vast green background of the canvas on the easel. "My girl friend is showing me how. She's a very good painter. Her husband was a famous young German Expressionist. She has a loft full of his paintings, must be worth thousands of dollars."

He stood there a short time, displaying the canvasses and talking about painting with a relish as green, perhaps, as the canvas on the easel, surprised that he could paint at all, surprised that anyone would compliment his paint-ings, surprised almost, that talent could be universal. But his business was with literature.

"See," he said, returning to the study, "Allen and Gregory—Gregory Corso—like they come up to me at midnight and say"—and he imitated Allen with an excited half-whisper—"and say, 'Look, we've done all this, we've made great literature. Why don't we do something REAL great and take over the WORLD!' And Gregory says, 'I'll be your HENCHMAN!' You know, half joking. I say, 'Yeah,'" and his voice cracked in innocent simplicity as he imitated himself saying Yeah—"but I just want to be Cervantes alone by candlelight. And they both say 'What would you do if you conquered the world, what would you do with it? It'll cough and won't let you sleep all night,' you know, quoting from *Howl*. And I really do want to go away, you know, in the country and spend long, long times just being an old Japanese haiku poet. An Emily Dickinson type man. I can't stand the hectic, public eye, you know. I like to go out and get stoned Saturday night with a gang of guys and girls, but I don't like the official connotations. But Allen and Gregory, they just love that. They'd love to be big . . . to be riding in green Chrysler squads and all that stuff. They'd love that. Gregory, he's kidding all the time . . . when he says that. And Allen . . . Allen is the sweetest man in the world! And I've thought about him for years as being the devil, see"—and he dropped his voice to mimic an inner one, speaking in a nervous, ominous undertone—" 'see, he's the devil, he's the devil' "—and then he raised it again, saying: "Sometimes I thought,"—and he dropped it once more—" 'No, I'm the devil.' But now we've both got older and I realize he's not the devil at all. I used to tell him, 'You're the devil.' He'd say, 'Don't talk like that!' Now I realize he's the sweetest . . .

"He doesn't drink much. He's had a lot of dope, you know. That guy's had more dope, heavy dope, you know, in the arm, than anyone I know that didn't become a dope addict. Great will power! Great will power! Experiments. I've had a lot, too. But I didn't have to use will power because I have an allergy to it. I keep throwing up. Yeah, I've had a lot. Not now, though. Like, I'll go to Tangier and see Bill Burroughs and he'll say, "Well, boy, how about kicking the gong around tonight and get some opium!' Or else I go to Mexico City and see old Bill Garver. He'll say, 'Well, I'll give you a shot of morphine.' "And he imitated Bill Garver with a Midwestern twang and then he imitated himself: " 'Okay, Bill.' . . . Well, what happens when you take it is you throw up. But after you throw up, you lay in the bed for eight hours, great for your mind. Great to get rid of your liver bile, too. Burroughs, he was 'Old Bull Lee' in *On the Road*. Actually, there was none of that gang who was really bad, except one guy named Phil. He was 'Mad Killer' in 1945. He used to kill storekeepers, but we didn't find out about that until later when he was arrested. He hanged himself in the Tombs."

He arose again from his chair and stepped to the dresser, where he pulled open another drawer. Inside were piles of notebooks, small, five-cent, pocket size, like the one protruding from his back pocket now, each pile with fifteen or twenty notebooks bound together with rubber bands, the piles in neat rows, one next to the other, filling the drawer.

"Novel," he said, tapping a pile, "novel," he said tapping another, "novel," he said, tapping a third, "novel," he said tapping a fourth, "novel, novel, novel," and he waved his had over the rest of the piles. "That's the way I write 'em—like that! See, Truman Capote said I always typewrite. I wrote half of them in pencil. Like *Visions of Neal*, my greatest book, right there. *Visions of Neal*. All in pencil. Here's *The Dharma Bums*"—and he pointed to a manuscript typewritten on a roll of teletype paper. "It's a hundred feet long. I wrote *On the Road* on another roll—on Cannastra's paper, a roll of

Cannastra's drawing paper that you draw through.[16] For *Dharma Bums* I could afford the teletype roll. Three dollars," and he laughed. "*On the Road*, I gave that roll to Viking. It was all no paragraphs, single-spaced—all one big paragraph. I had to retype it so they could publish it. Do people realize what an anguish it is to write an original story three hundred pages long?

"See, I changed my style from *The Town and the City* because of Neal—Neal Cassady. Because of a forty-thousand-word letter that Neal wrote me. He wrote me a forty-thousand-word letter! But Allen lost the letter, or Gerd Stern did, actually. Gerd Stern, he lived on a barge in Sausalito. He lost that great letter, which was a work of literary genius. Neal, he was just telling me what happened one time in Denver, and he had every detail. It was just like Dostoyevsky. And I realized that's the way to tell a story—just tell it! I really got it from Neal. So I started to tell the story just the way it happened, too. *The Town and the City* was fiction, you know, mostly. But in spontaneous prose, you just tell what happened. You don't stop, you just keep going. That's

16. See note #1, Beat.
Final note: "In any case, apparently what Allen wants you to do is to abandon this project entirely but it's too late. So in putting in these inserts, corrections, additions and deletions I'm doing the best I can do to promote a hopelessly committed venture. I want you to know that in discussing Cassady, Ginsberg, Burroughs, myself, Orlovsky and Corso you're dealing with some great American writers, the greatest since the Transcendentalists (Thoreau, Emerson, Whitman, Dickinson) and your name will go down with us or up with us. You will go 'up'! You must realize that what we mean by 'shallow journalism' is simply the failure to give complete tragic detail to your facts for the sake of 'sensational touches.' These 'sensational touches' are only sensational today, not tomorrow, when a posterity will want to know every detail and fact of this our sad life today. You know for instance that I, as author of *Doctor Sax*, am no clown-drunkard merely. That I am a man of stature which will be recognized when the dust settles. A lot of jealous critics hate us, you know that. Corso and Burroughs have produced tremendously great work. You've got to give them your loving attention when you talk about them. A certain party does seem to put poor Allen Ginsberg in a silly light. If he grabbed a Harper girl by the neck I'm sure there was a certain charm in the way he did it, which you don't mention at all. You make him look like a hood. Why? Did Wechsler ask you to do a hatchet job on the beat generation on account of I called him a shit at Hunter College? Is that why? Are you truly sad and repentant when you come into Allen's kitchen and apologize or is that just your technique to get the story? Are you just buttering these young struggling artists (including myself) in order to make fools of them? If so, your reward will not be huge. In fact I can expose you in my Escapade column any time. But I think you're sincere and what you say about journalistic stringencies is accurate. I don't know. The whole thing has been a sad mess, that young kids in this country instead of yearning to be jet pilots should have turned their attention to Rimbaud and Shakespeare and struggled to draw their breath in pain to tell a brother's story.

—Jean Louis"

the way Neal wrote me the letter. You get excited in telling a story, like Homer probably did. Spontaneity is also in Shakespeare, you know. His publishers say that all his manuscripts were brought in—he brought them in clean, without a mark, without a change, without an addition, without an erasure. They said that he was such a perfect writer, that he just flowed right along. I believe it. Nobody can prove it, but that's what I think. I can tell by the swing and rhythm of his speeches. So, I get this from Neal, I wrote *On the Road* about Neal. He was the prototype for Dean Moriarty in *On the Road*.

"Neal . . . Neal was discovered by Denver Doll, by the guy who was the prototype for Denver Doll in *On the Road*. But Malcolm Cowley made me take him all out of the book," and he laughed. "Because he's a lawyer. He's the guy who developed Neal, see? He discovered Neal. Neal was an urchin. It's a real Charlie Chaplin story, and he's a real Charlie Chaplin. Yeah! Justin W. Brierly"—and he pronounced Justin W. Brierly as if he were sitting in a Midwest Elk's Club with a large cigar in his mouth. "He's a lawyer. That's why they were afraid of him at Viking. He went to one of his clients who was a drunken Indian. Knocked on the door, and the door was opened by a fifteen-year-old boy with a big hard-on. Neal. Screwing the maid upstairs. Denver Doll said, 'Well, what is this?' "—and he imitated the voice with the cigar in his mouth—"He said, 'My dear fellow,' he said, 'your ears aren't washed.' Took him home and made him wash his ears. Made him go to school. Made him read literature. Made him read Schopenhauer. See? Wrote long letters to Neal's warden in reform school. We see now that he was a wise, perceptive man to believe in Neal.

"So this guy, who is a member of the Columbia Alumni Association, see, this Denver Doll, the old lawyer, he was going to get Neal into Columbia. And Denver Doll kept coming to New York on big trips to see Hall Chase, Ed White and all the Columbia boys, and there was Ginsberg and Kerouac hanging around Hall Chase and Ed White, the Phi Beta Kappa scholar. So, rumors of Neal began floating around, and he finally came. Quite a story, at that! Completely complicated by Dostoyevsky."

Outside the sun was ice and twilight, and he began changing his clothes, putting on a pair of slacks, a sport shirt and a jacket. He walked downstairs and his mother made him put on a tie as well, a Continental bow tie, the latest style then, and she had bought it for him as a gift.

"See," she said, "I told you he has new clothes. He wears them sometimes," and she smiled again.

He kissed her goodbye, it was time to go, he had an appointment in New York, and he was getting a ride. The author of *On the Road* didn't own a car.

"See," he said outside, "I'm going to move to Florida, close to my sister. I want my mother to be close to someone when I'm not home, when I'm traveling. When I'm traveling. When I'm on the road. Like tonight, I'll go away, I'll be away all weekend, and my mother will be home alone in that big house. She gets frightened. I don't like to think of her home alone there . . ."

He fingered his bow tie. Later, when he got to New York, he took it off in a barroom.

"But Neal," he said, "Neal knows me better than anybody else. Neal knows way down deep what I really am. See, Neal is more like Dostoyevsky, he's a sex fiend like Dostoyevsky, he writes like Dostoyevsky. I got my rhythm from Neal, that's the way he talks, Okie rhythms. Like"—and he imitated, perhaps Neal Cassady, perhaps himself—"Like, 'Now, look h'yar, boy, I'm gonna tell you what see? You hear me boy?'—That's the way he talks. I've written three novels about Neal and a play—*On the Road*, *Visions of Neal*, and *Desolation Angels* and 'Beat Generations,' that's the play, we're making a little movie out of the third act. Called 'Pull My Daisy.' Neal . . . Neal was a great Midwest Poolroom Saint. Neal Cassady and I love each other greatly."

What Is the Beat Generation?

Val Duncan / 1959

From *Newsday*, August 4, 1959, p. 15C. Reprinted with permission.

If the Beat Generation acknowledges any leader at all, it is Jack Kerouac, author and prophet. A look at him is an insight into the phenomenon we call the Beat Generation.

His shirt tail flops out over the back of faded and tattered dungarees. He slouches against a fence on the quiet Northport street, waiting for a bus to take him to the shopping center. But the bus could pass him by because his head is bent in concentration as he scribbles with the stub of a pencil in a wrinkled and weary little notebook.

You offer him a ride and he doesn't say thanks. Just: "Durn it. Left my wallet home. Could you lend me a couple of bucks? Have to get some milk, just a few things." He sprawls over the seat of the car, his eyes far away, waiting to be delivered to the store.

A bum? No, but you couldn't be blamed for thinking so. He's Jack Kerouac. He's beat—and more. He's the king of the beats. A million copies of his books have hit the bookshelves. One came out this spring. The latest went on display last week. Like his runaway best sellers, *On the Road* and *The Dharma Bums*, they tell of his flight from civilization, the highways, the ships, the mountains—any remoteness where an unhappy and restless soul can escape the tensions of the world today.

As the documentation of a dissafiliate, the Kerouac books are on the "must" lists of all who are beat or hope to be. They comprise a sort of Baedeker of beatism, leading the novice in search of his Self down tortuous literary paths, past mystic visions of transcending beauty and a sprinkling of four-letter words.

Kerouac, the leading novelist amid a spate of beat poets, has tried to find his Self (call it Dharma, Enlightenment—God, if you will) through action and meditation. The action put him in the Columbia varsity backfield, on a

37

ship to the Arctic, in a Northwest forest with an ax in his hand, riding the rails and htichhiking 10,000 miles by rule of thumb.

The meditation sent him to dusty shelves for books on Buddhism, Zen, and the works of Villon, Thoreau and Whitman. And he filled a dozen notebooks with carefully inscribed Orienal notes and verses.

Little wonder then that, despite his tatters, the man himself and his letters cause shivers of excitement among the young beats that throng the espresso houses from Greenwich Village to North Beach in San Francisco.

But they no longer excite him. The man who has been lionized by everyone everywhere from Mexican peons to Manhattan penthouses is tired of people.

"You have to be alone to think and write. Northport is too noisy. I have to get away. In the end I want to be a hermit, living on a mountainside. Nobody around but deer. Write all week, go down to the village for food and fun on Saturday nights."

He's been married twice, and, "That's enough for me. One wife put on too much pressure: 'Get up and mow the lawn.' The other wife, all I could feed her was mayonnaise sandwiches. She went home. She was hungry."

But hunger never sent Kerouac home. On the road he dug spuds for slumgullion, chomped raw carrots and slept on moss. He picked up friends on the way, seeking what he sought, young men and women who roamed wide, tasting the bitter sweets of life and listening to the rain, the birds and the crickets—the biggest juke in the world.

"No fiction," says Kerouac. "I wrote what really happened."

He peopled his books with the cool cats and the chicks he found along the way. Some of them became writers and co-apostles with Kerouac in the beat movement.

There was Allen Ginsberg, now the leading beat poet who was the Carlo Marx of *On the Road*. There was Gary Snyder, the irrepressible, earthy hero of the *Dharma Bums*, who is now studying for the Buddhist priesthood in Japan. There was Neal Cassady, the Dean Moriarity of *On the Road*, who now wants Kerouac to send him a typewriter so he can write about San Quentin, where he is serving a marijuana rap. Two girls, Marylou and Camille, both of whom married Cassady, danced and cried their way through the Kerouac saga.

Kerouac's description of the monumental mountain party the night before Snyder left for Japan is a highlight of *The Dharma Bums*. The leap of the campfire flames, the flow of wine, the Oriental love rite of yabyum, the sweet, taut reaching of youth for the unreachable. And the author sadly goes out into the forest knowing that it is all of the moment, and the moment has gone. It will rain before dawn and his friends will leave.

Such moods of soft despair are woven with the bursts of anger and frenzied joy in the beat writings. The keynote of sadness seems to be a beat's yearning to find in his Self the happiness that cannot be found in a world where he sees more evil than good.

Ginsberg (the Carlo Marx designation, says Kerouac, was to honor Groucho, and had no political connotation) has put his finger on this when he discussed his bestseller poem *Howl.*

Ginsberg says the poem, which some have called blasphemous, was written in the cadence of a Hebraic chant, such as were set down by the biblical prophets. Kerouac, says the author, named the poem *Howl* and the name was right.

"That's what it's supposed to represent," he said. "Prophets howling in the wilderness. That, in fact, is what the whole beat generation is, if it's anything, prophets howling against a crazy civilzation."

If Kerouac is king of the beats, then Ginsberg is the poet laureate. And Gregory Corso, now twenty-eight, who saw the inside of several jails for petty thefts before he was twenty, is the heir presumptive. In a recently published volume, *The Bomb*, Corso addresses the hydrogen nemesis: "Bomb, you are as cruel as man makes you, and you're no crueler than cancer."

This kind of verse and others are being read nightly in the beat pads and coffeehouses against a background of modern jazz. It's the beat of a generation.

Playing "Baseball" with Jack Kerouac

Stan Isaacs / 1961

From *Newsday*, February 17, 1961, p. 16C. Reprinted with permission.

The snow was a few feet deep outside, but the cry of the hot dog vendor and the crack of the warm-up ball against the catcher's mitt sounded inside writer Jack Kerouac's house in Northport recently as the Pittsburgh Browns prepared to take the field against the visiting Chicago Blues in a battle for fifth place.

Chicago manager Cracker Jack Kerouac chose the Blues' curve-balling righty Larry Hooker to protect the Blues' one-game lead over the Browns. Pants Isaacs, sometime reporter filling in for ailing Pittsburgh manager Pic Tibbs, countered with his young ace, hard-luck Ron Melaney.

"Melaney has a blazing fast ball," Kerouac said. "I created him the same night I unveiled Bob Cold of the league-leading Cincinnati Blacks. Cold is the fastest pitcher in the league, and has an 11–4 record with a 2.36 earned-run average." While the fans in Plymouth Stadium awaited the cry of "play ball," Kerouac—the low priest of the beat generation—sketched in some background on his baseball game.

He manipulates it with a set of home-made cards. It is a game he has used in some of his short stories, and he hopes to put it on the market some day. "I usually play it alone when I'm in the woods," he said as he made up a box score in the official league stenographic notebook.

Kerouac's league is full of great players. There's El Negro of the St. Louis Whites, the leading home run hitter. ("He's a big Negro from Latin America," Kerouac said. " 'El Negro' means 'The Negro.' ") There's Wino Love of the Detroit Reds, the league's leading hitter with a .344 average. ("He's called 'Wino' because he drinks, but he's still a great hitter.") Big Bill Louis is everybody's favorite. ("I patterned him after Babe Ruth: one day I had him come to bat chewing on a frankfurter.") Pic Jackson, the league's best hitting pitcher, likes to read the Sunday supplement, and his name "Pic" is short for Pictorial Review.

Kerouac turned over the first card and Melaney's first pitch was a strike. Ron quickly retired Chicago's first two hitters, the Simms brothers. "Sonny Simms, the center fielder, is like Willy Mays," Kerouac said. "His younger brother, Sugar Ray, was just brought up from the minors. He's called Sugar Ray because he is a flashy character and looks like Sugar Ray Robinson.") With two out, Melaney walked Byrd Duff and Earl Morrison, a tall left-handed batter with eye-glasses, sent him home with a double to left.

Pittsburgh came back with a run in its half. Burlingame Japes celebrated his return to the lineup by starting the rally with a walk. "Japes," Kerouac said, "is forty years old now, a little left-handed hitter who in his younger days was the league base-stealing champ. I put him in for Joe Boston who broke his leg sliding and who wasn't helping the team anyway." Slugger Herb Jangraw singled Japes to second. Then a walk to catcher Herm Bigger loaded the bases. ("Bigger is a Roy Campanella type. He thinks there's nothing better than comfortable shoes and a good mattress.) The run scored as Hooker walked John Gronning on four pitches.

Manager Isaas talked to Melaney before the second inning and Ron proceeded to pitch four scoreless innings. In the meantime, the Pittsburgh Browns pecked away at Hooker for a 3–1 lead.

Chicago scored again in the sixth as Morrison singled, stole second and scored on a triple by Francis X. Cudley. ("He's an Irishman from Boston. He stands up at the plate very erect, like a Jesuit.")

Pittsburgh came back in its half on a two-run homer by Gronning. ("That's what makes the game so good; he's only a .200 hitter but even he can come through.") The Browns then added four more in the seventh on a rally that started when Cudley messed up a grounder by Keggs. ("Keggs is an old guy; his neck is seared from the Arkansas sun. He has a brother named Earl who used to be a ball player, but who now is back in Texarkana selling hardware.")

The rally continued with Melaney's second hit and a two-run double by Lefty Murphree that knocked out Hooker and brought on Hugh Nesbitt, a six-foot-seven relief specialist. An error by Sugar Ray, trying to showboat a grounder, and a third hit by Jangraw upped the Browns' lead to 9–2.

Simms atoned for the error by homering in the eighth, but Melaney bore down after that, striking out three of the last five hitters. The last out was a grounder to shortstop by pinch-hitter Hophead Dean. "Some people think he's called 'Hophead' because he takes pot, but actually it's because he wears his hat askew and does silly things," Kerouac said.

It was a good game.

Pittsburgh Browns (9)	AB	R	H
Lefty Murphree, cf	6	1	2
Burlingame Japes, rf	5	2	0
Herb Jangraw, lf	5	1	3
Hank Melanus, 1b	5	0	1
Herm Bigger, c	4	0	1
John Gronning, 2b	4	2	2
Rayvon Beck, 3b	5	0	1
Johnny Keggs, ss	5	2	3
Ron Melaney, p	3	1	2
Totals	42	9	15
Chicago Blues (3)	AB	R	H
Sonny Simms, cf	4	0	1
Sugar Ray Simms, 1b	4	1	1
Byrd Duffy, rf	3	1	1
Earl Morrison, lf	4	1	2
Francis X. Cudley, ss	4	0	2
Don Jungs, 2b	4	0	0
a-Duke Wilder	1	0	0
Hank Dasse, c	4	0	0
Larry Hooker, p	3	0	0
Hugh Nesbitt, p	0	0	0
b-Hophead Dean	1	0	0
Totals	35	3	8

a-Struck out for Jungs in 9th. b-Grounded out for Nesbitt in 9th

Chicago——— 100	001	010—3	5	2
Pittsburgh—— 111	002	40x—9	15	0

E—R Simms, Cudley. RBI—Morrison, Cudley, R. Simms, Gronning 3, Japes, Melaney, Murphree 2, Bigger, Jangraw. Left—Chicago 5, Pittsburgh 14 2B—Morrison, Melaney 3B—Cudley, Murphree. HR—R. Simms, Gronning. SB—Mirrison, Jangraw.

	IP	H	R	ER	BB	SO
Melaney (W, 6–7)	9	8	3	3	1	6
Hooker (L, 3–5)	6	12	9	7	5	7
Nesbitt	2	3	0	0	0	0

I Simply Plan a Completely Written Lifetime

Anonymous / 1963

From *Chicago Daily News*, August 24, 1963, *Panorama* sec., p. 8.

A new book by Jack Kerouac, once considered the prime spokesman for the Beat Generation, is to be published next month. Its title is *Visions of Gerard* (Farrar, Straus & Co.) and its subject matter—dealing, among other things, with Catholicism—prompted a recent interviewer to ask some pertinent questions.

Q: At first glance, the Catholicism in *Visions of Gerard* seems to be something new for you. Is it?
A: Catholicism in my books is not a new tack for me. Actually, there was some Catholicism in *The Dharma Bums* which the publishers saw fit to delete. There's a lot of Catholicism in *Big Sur*, in *Lonesome Traveler*, and even more in *Tristessa*, and a running brief on the subject in *Maggie Cassidy*. My first novel, *The Town and the City*, was essentially a Catholic story. The "beat" theme in the hepcat books like *On the Road* and *The Subterraneans* is not opposed to Catholicism. I'm born a Catholic and it's nothing new with me.

At home or abroad, I always carry my rosary more or less for good luck. Most of the amateur painting I've done is of pietas, crucifixions, saints, and I have a nice collection of sacred music. I always give my stories and poems free to *Jubilee Magazine* as a contribution to the Church. I was baptized, received First Communion and feel quite calm about the whole thing.

Q: How was *Visions of Gerard* written?
A: *Visions of Gerard* was written at the kitchen table of my sister's home in Big Easonburg Woods, North Carolina, over a ten-night stretch, midnight to dawn, ending with refreshing visits to the piney barrens out behind the

cotton field at sunrise. I did no rewriting or revising whatever, except for name changes and one important comma finally inserted somewhere, where I'd made a spontaneous mistake about it being needed, although I did reject a whole night's writing and started all over again on the section the next night. It was all written by hand, in pencil, in little notebooks. Certain kinds of stories seem to deny the rackety typewriter.

Q: *Visions of Gerard* is part of the series you call the Duluoz Legend. What are your future plans for that?
A: Future plans for the Duluoz Legend are to fill in the gaps left open in the chronological past. The sequel to *The Dharma Bums* is already written (called *Desolation Angels*) and the sequel to that (already written) is called *Passing Through*. The sequel to *Visions of Gerard* (not yet written) will be called *Vanity of Duluoz* and then come the post–*Big Sur* adventures of my future life, whatever it will be, if any.

The final scope of the Legend will be simply a completely written lifetime with all its hundreds of characters and events and levels interswirling and reappearing and becoming complete, somewhat a la Balzac and Proust. But each section, that is, each novel, has to stand by itself as an individual story with a flavor of its own and a pivot of its own. Nevertheless, they must all fit together on one shelf as a continuous tale.

Q: The setting for *Visions of Gerard* is your home town of Lowell. When were you last there?
A: In October 1962 and I got a big "celebrity" reception and had to run away back to New York. I'm sort of a hero there. Much fun. The people there, old football cronies, cousins, friends, new acquaintances, old newspaper confreres, the teaching fraternity, gossips, characters all realize I just go there to bask and drink but we really have great rapports and I'm going back there soon because there are more books in that little Christian city than you could have packed in Carthage. A golden Byzantine dome rises from the roofs along the canal; a Gothic copy of Chartres rises from the slums of Moody Street; little children speak French, Greek, Polish and even Portuguese on their way to school. And I have a recurrent dream of simply walking around the deserted twilight streets of Lowell, in the mist, eager to turn every known and fabled corner. A very eerie, recurrent dream, but it always makes me happy when I wake up.

Q: In a recent magazine article, a writer says the Beats are no longer on the road, "that even Kerouac—their god—had settled down on Long Island with his mother." Do you accept that?

A: I've always been "settled with my mother" who supported me by working in shoe factories while I wrote most of my books years ago. She's my friend as well as my mother. When I go on the road I always have a quiet, clean home to come back to, and to work in, which probably accounts for the fact that I've published twelve books in the last six years.

Kerouac Revisited
Val Duncan / 1964

From *Newsday*, July 18, 1964, pp. 8W–9W. Reprinted with permission.

He sits in the rocking chair, a can of beer in his hand. His eyes are startlingly blue and they seem to be staring through the walls. Behind the shag of a black, four-day beard, there's a friendly, honest face with a ready smile.

"Look," he says, bending to his sockless feet, encased in a pair of ragged red slippers. He points to callouses on each ankle. "That's from doing so much rocking. Hours of it. How about a shot of Scotch?"

Here is Jack Kerouac, so-called bard of the Beat Generation, the spokesman for the cool cats and their chicks, the guru of the pad dwellers from Greenwich Village to the Coast. His books, hard and soft covers, have sold in the millions and have been translated into twelve languages.

He spots the photographer and fingers the heavy stubble on his face. "If you're going to take pictures, I'd better get rid of this." He goes off to shave, nicking his cheek in the process. He comes back. You ask him how he's doing these days.

"Come with me," he says, and beer can and shot glass in either hand, leads the way down the corridor of the $24,000 house he owns at 7 Judy Ann Court, Northport. The room has a thousand books on many shelves—and everybody's there from Aristophanes to Allen Ginsberg. Two of the walls blaze with abstract paintings and bright postcards from many lands. Classics, primitives, El Greco, Rouault, Picasso, Van Gogh, Rousseau, Gaugin—and many more, contrasting with oriental plaques and soft Japanese mezzotints. Special spotlights stab down at his typewriter. He spins a dial and an expensive hi-fi blasts into action. It is far-out jazz.

"Now," he says, carefully placing his drinks on coasters so that no stains will mar his books or papers. Then he takes off one of his slippers, centers it precisely in the center of the floor, puts his head down on it and, with the grace of a champion gymnast, elevates his feet until he is standing on his head. Then with continuingly perfect form he raises and lowers his feet ten times. The rippling stomach muscles show the strain—and the strength.

But when it's over he's not even breathing hard. "See," he says, draining his shot glass. "That's how I'm doing these days."

He flexes bulging biceps and slaps his belly, hard as a butcher block. Kerouac, at forty-two, stands five feet, eight inches, weighs 190 pounds without an ounce of fat. It's the kind of body you need to do the things he's done—played varsity football for Columbia, sailed the Arctic run during the war, thumbed his way from coast to coast, rode the rods to the Northwest where he axed down trees.

It was the telling of his travels across the country and Europe that won him the idolization of five million youngsters, hipsters, poets, jazzmen, and rich girls in convertibles. In his books, they lived vicariously as free souls, roaming the earth, shunning civilization—and its responsibilities—reading books on Zen Buddhism, trying to find their Inner Self.

And, in him, too, despite his physical strength, they perceived an essential gentleness about him. He is not a hard man. Though he has been drinking heavily, his eyes remain clear, with a purity about it, and his great fist is firm in the handshake.

"Never hit anybody in my life," he says. "Had to slap a guy when he started bothering another smaller guy. Just slapped him with both palms—not hard, just enough to shake him back to sense."

On impulse, he suddenly snaps off the blasting hi-fi. The ensuing silence is deafening. He calls out to his mother in a foreign tongue that sounds vaguely like French. And a few seconds later a dimple-faced little old lady appears, studying him worriedly through her glasses. "It's your one fault, Jack," she says. "Too much you drink." She sighs but hands him another can of beer.

"Now for the Russian," he says, and he changes tapes. He does this fast because although he has dozens of tapes he can find any one instantly by an index system of cards, coded with stars, moons, crosses, crescents and other symbols. He invented the system and here is another facet of the mercurial Kerouac—a passion for orderliness. He can lay his hand on any book immediately. His thousands of letters and papers are neatly filed and indexed in a metal cabinet.

Again the machine blasts forth. It is Shostakovich's Fifth. Kerouac taps his feet, smashes his hands on the skinhead of a conga drum. Then he whirls into a dance and it is almost classical ballet—the arabesque, entrechat, pirouette. He's good at it. He makes a lot of funny faces. He stops and cocks an ear to the music. "Listen to the pain and sweetness of it," he says. He gulps beer.

"My mother," he says. "I take good care of her. She speaks to me in English but I talk medieval French to her. It is the language of François Villon," and knowing its exact position on the shelf, he whips down a copy of the French poet's works. "Great stuff, but Shakespeare was the best of them all and after him James Joyce." He flourishes five-pound volumes of *Ulysses* and *Finnegans Wake*.

His reference to Villon and old French brings him close to a topic that is almost a fetish with him—the study of national origins, names, pronunciations and a mystical belief that he has lived other lives before this.

"My family is five thousand years old," he says. "People bug me. They say what the hell kind of a name is Kerouac, anyway? It's easy. Just a real old Irish name—Keltic. 'Ker' means house in Keltic. 'Ouac' means 'on the moor.' But my family traveled far. They started in Ireland, traveled to Wales, then Cornwall, then Brittany, where they learned the old French, then four hundred years ago to Canada. Did you know that one of the Iroquois nations is named Kerouac?"

He strikes a dramatic pose and you're not sure if he's kidding. "Once I was Tristan looking for Isolde and once I rode the plains of Tartary on a shaggy pony." He tells of a friend he bummed around with on the Coast who said that everyone has lived twenty or thirty lives before. "He's a funny guy but he might be right."

His mention of friends brings up the question of what's happening in the World of Beatism. Nobody has heard much about it lately. But he doesn't like the question, evades it, says: "It's time to sing a song." But you insist, repeat the question.

He shrugs. "They're still reading poetry but I never get to the Village any more." (Where once he could command $200 for a single poetry reading.) "They don't like me. All the old timers are turning politicians, getting up petitions for civil rights and all that kind of stuff. It's politics, not art any more."

Though Kerouac may not have changed, in his eyes the old world of bumming the country with pot-smoking hipsters and pickup chicks, learning how to make tequila from cactus and practicing oriental love rites, seems to be taking a new direction. "There's more money around." He won't say how much his books have brought but he said he'd guessed he paid out "about $15,000" in agency fees since 1957 when his classic *On the Road* vaulted him to fame. Agents normally receive a 10 percent commission.

Though none of his later books equaled *On the Road*, all sold well, particularly *Dharma Bums*. His last two books, *Big Sur* and *Visions of Gerard*, both published by Farrar, Straus Inc., are big sellers and in constant demand at libraries. Most of his books tell pretty much the same story—booze-filled wanderings of young people amid the beauty and misery of life. Many of the characters are the same, but for legal reasons he has not been allowed to repeat their names. However, the thread is there: young love, sex, drugs, an endless odyssey in search of self ("call it Dharma, Enlightenment—God if you will").

In his studies of Zen, search for Self and other unconventionalities, Kerouac sees no conflict with being a Roman Catholic. Over his bed hangs a rosary.

"Know what I do every night?" Reverently he tiptoes over to the beads, gently picks up the Crucifix and presses it to his lips. "The silent kiss," he says. "Every night."

But every night is not the same. Some nights he drinks. Some nights he works. He has two books in the making, with commissions for articles for several slick magazines. His essay on Shakespeare that appeared in a top show business magazine earlier this year received critical acclaim, not because it was written in the usual razmataz semi-gibberish of beat writing, but because it was a highly polished treatise, richly phrased and displaying a profundity of scholarship. He also writes prefaces for art books and completed a narration for a movie short.

"I need quiet to work," he says, gazing out on a lawn that he has had made into a small grotto, the whole area surrounded by a stout, six-foot fence of Alaska cedar planking. "Self- protection. People always bugging me. Once a guy crashed in at five in the morning and screamed: 'Are you busy?'"

When Kerouac types, he does it fast. Truman Capote once said: "He's not a writer, he's a typewriter." Once started, he doesn't stop, using long rolls of paper instead of individual sheets. "Just blast away. Waste no time fooling with paper. Write a book without stopping." He covers all of his paper— single space, with margins of only one eighth of an inch.

At present, he's working on the draft of a story called "Memory Babe," set near the Canadian border, an area of nostalgia for Massachusetts-born Kerouac. "My grandfather, Jean-Baptiste, lived up there. He taught me the importance of the rocking chair." His other work probably will be titled "An American Passed Here," recollections of adventures in Europe and North Africa.

Despite the fence and the quiet of his little side street, it's still "too noisy." He's selling his house here and moving to Florida. After that he's off to Europe—"maybe Russia, too. I hate communism but I'd like to see the country."

Out of it all he believes will come another book—or as he is beginning to see it, another long chapter to be used in a future masterwork. This would be known as the Duluoz Legend that he intends to write "in my old age and then die happy."

He explains this by quoting from his preface in *Big Sur*, in which he compares this future compilation with the works of Proust "except that my remembrances are written on the run instead of a sick bed . . . the whole thing forms an enormous comedy, seen through the eyes of poor Ti Jean (me), otherwise known as Jack Duluoz, the world of raging action and folly and also of gentle sweetness seen through the keyhole of his eye."

Kerouac squints out the window at the setting sun. It is the time when most people are thinking of dinner.

"Drop me off downtown," he says. "I'm out of Scotch and I need a shot."

You let him off at a local bar. He shuffles inside, shirttail flapping, still in his tattered slippers. He doesn't know what will happen next and doesn't seem to care. At the bar he may find quiet oblivion—or a new character to write about.

The Art of Fiction:
Jack Kerouac

Ted Berrigan / 1967

From *The Paris Review*, 11, no. 43 (1968): 60–105. Reprinted by permission of *The Paris Review.* Copyright © 1968 *The Paris Review.*

Jack Kerouac is now forty-five years old. His thirteenth novel, *Vanity of Duluoz* was published earlier this year. He lives with his wife of one year, Stella, and his invalid mother in a brick ranch-style house in a residential district of Lowell, Massachusetts, the city in which he spent all of his childhood. The Kerouacs have no telephone. Ted Berrigan had contacted Kerouac some months earlier and persuaded him to do the interview. When he felt the time had come for their meeting to take place, he simply showed up at the Kerouacs' house. Two friends, poets Aram Saroyan and Duncan McNaughton, accompanied him. Kerouac answered his ring; Berrigan quickly told him his name and the visit's purpose. Kerouac welcomed the poets, but before he could show them in, his wife, a very determined woman, seized him from behind and told the group to leave at once.

"Jack and I began talking simultaneously, saying 'Paris Review!' 'Interview!' etc.," Berrigan recalls, "while Duncan and Aram began to slink back toward the car. All seemed lost, but I kept talking in what I hoped was a civilized, reasonable, calming and friendly tone of voice, and soon Mrs. Kerouac agreed to let us in for twenty minutes, on the condition that there be no drinking.

"Once inside, as it became evident that we actually were in pursuit of a serious purpose, Mrs. Kerouac became more friendly, and we were able to commence the interview. It seems that people still show up constantly at the Kerouacs' looking for the author of *On the Road,* and stay for days, drinking all the liquor and diverting Jack from his serious occupations.

"As the evening progressed the atmosphere changed considerably, and Mrs. Kerouac, Stella, proved a gracious and charming hostess. The most amazing thing about Jack Kerouac is his magic voice, which sounds exactly like his

51

works, and is capable of the most astounding and disconcerting changes in no time flat. It dictates everything, including this interview.

"After the interview, Kerouac, who had been sitting throughout the interview in a President Kennedy–type rocker, moved over to a big poppa chair, and said, 'So you boys are poets, hey? Well, let's hear some of your poetry.' We stayed for about an hour longer, and Aram and I read some of our things. Finally, he gave each of us a signed broadside of a recent poem of his, and we left."

Some portions of this interview have been filled out with Kerouac's written replies to questions put to him subsequent to the interview. It was felt these additions would add substance to the portrait of the author and his métier.

Interviewer: Could we put the footstool over here to put this on?
Stella: Yes.
Kerouac: God, you're so inadequate there, Berrigan.

Interviewer: Well, I'm no tape-recorder man, Jack. I'm just a big talker, like you. O.K., we're off.
Kerouac: O.K.? (*Whistles*) O.K.?

Interviewer: Actually I'd like to start . . . the first book I ever read by you, oddly enough, since most people first read *On the Road* . . . the first one I read was *The Town and the City* . . .
Kerouac: Gee!

Interviewer: I checked it out of the library . . .
Kerouac: Gee! . . . Did you read *Dr. Sax*? . . . *Tristessa*? . . .

Interviewer: You better believe it. I even read *Rimbaud*. I have a copy of *Visions of Cody* that Ron Padgett bought in Tulsa, Oklahoma.
Kerouac: Screw Ron Padgett! You know why? He started a little magazine called *White Dove Review* in Kansas City, was it? Tulsa? Oklahoma . . . yes. He wrote, Start our magazine off by sending us a great big poem. So I sent him the "Thrashing Doves." And then I sent him another one and he rejected the second one because his magazine was already started. That's to show you how punks try to make their way by scratching down on a man's back. Aw, he's no poet. You know who's a great poet? I know who the great poets are.

Interviewer: Who?

Kerouac: Let's see, is it . . . William Bissette of Vancouver. An Indian boy. Bill Bissette, or Bissonnette.

Saroyan: Let's talk about Jack Kerouac.

Kerouac: He's not better than Bill Bissette, but he's very original.

Interviewer: Why don't we begin with editors. How do you . . .

Kerouac: O.K. All my editors since Malcolm Cowley have had instructions to leave my prose exactly as I wrote it. In the days of Malcolm Cowley, with *On the Road* and *The Dharma Bums*, I had no power to stand by my style for better or for worse. When Malcolm Cowley made endless revisions and inserted thousands of needless commas like, say, Cheyenne, Wyoming (why not just say Cheyenne Wyoming and let it go at that, for instance), why, I spent $500 making the complete restitution of the *Bums* manuscript and got a bill from Viking Press called "Revisions." Ha ho ho. And so you asked about how do I work with an editor . . . well nowadays I am just grateful to him for his assistance in proofreading the manuscript and in discovering logical errors, such as dates, names of places. For instance in my last book I wrote Firth of Forth then looked it up, on the suggestion of my editor, and found that I'd really sailed off the Firth of Clyde. Things like that. Or I spelled Aleister Crowley "Alisteir," or he discovered little mistakes about the yardage in football games . . . and so forth. By not revising what you've already written you simply give the reader the actual workings of your mind during the writing itself: you confess your thoughts about events in your own unchangeable way . . . well, look, did you ever hear a guy telling a long wild tale to a bunch of men in a bar and all are listening and smiling, did you ever hear that guy stop to revise himself, go back to a previous sentence to improve it, to defray its rhythmic thought impact . . . If he pauses to blow his nose, isn't he planning his next sentence? And when he lets that next sentence loose, isn't it once and for all the way he wanted to say it? Doesn't he depart the thought of that sentence and, as Shakespeare says, "forever holds his tongue" on the subject, since he's passed over it like a part of the river flows over a rock once and for all and never returns and can never flow any other way in time? Incidentally, as for my bug against periods, that was for the prose in *October in the Railroad Earth,* very experimental, intended to clack along all the way like a steam engine pulling a hundred-car freight with a talky caboose at the end, that was my way at the time and it still can be done if the thinking during the swift writing is confessional and pure and all excited with the life of it. And be sure of this, I spent my entire youth writing slowly with revisions and endless re-hashing speculation and deleting and got so I was writing one sentence a day and the sentence had no FEELING. Goddamn it, FEELING is what I like in art, not CRAFTINESS and the hiding of feelings.

Interviewer: What encouraged you to use the "spontaneous" style of *On the Road*?

Kerouac: I got the idea for the spontaneous style of *On the Road* from seeing how good old Neal Cassady wrote his letters to me, all first person, fast, mad, confessional, completely serious, all detailed, with real names in his case however (being letters). I remembered also Goethe's admonition, well Goethe's prophecy that the future literature of the West would be confessional in nature; also Dostoevsky prophesied as much and might have started in on that if he'd lived long enough to do his projected masterwork, *The Great Sinner.* Cassady also began his early youthful writing with attempts at slow, painstaking, and-all-that-crap craft business, but got sick of it like I did, seeing it wasn't getting out his guts and heart the way it *felt* coming out. But I got the flash from his style. It's a cruel lie for those West Coast punks to say that I got the idea of *On the Road* from him. All his letters to me were about his younger days before I met him, a child with his father, et cetera, and about his later teenage experiences. The letter he sent me is erroneously reported to be a 13,000 word letter . . . no, the 13,000 word piece was his novel *The First Third,* which he kept in his possession. The letter, the main letter I mean, was 40,000 words long, mind you, a whole short novel. It was the greatest piece of writing I ever saw, better'n anybody in America, or at least enough to make Melville, Twain, Dreiser, Wolfe, I dunno who, spin in their graves. Allen Ginsberg asked me to lend him this vast letter so he could read it. He read it, then loaned it to a guy called Gerd Stern who lived on a houseboat in Sausalito, California, in 1955, and this fellow lost the letter: overboard I presume. Neal and I called it, for convenience, the *Joan Anderson Letter* . . . all about a Christmas weekend in the poolhalls, hotel rooms and jails of Denver, with hilarious events thoughout and tragic too, even a drawing of a window, with measurements to make the reader understand, all that. Now listen: this letter would have been printed under Neal's copyright, if we could find it, but as you know, it was my property as a letter to me, so Allen shouldn't have been so careless with it, nor the guy on the houseboat. If we can unearth this entire 40,000 word letter Neal shall be justified. We also did so much fast talking between the two of us, on tape recorders, way back in 1952, and listened to them so much, we both got the secret of LINGO in telling a tale and figured that was the only way to express the speed and tension and ecstatic tomfoolery of the age. . . . Is that enough?

Interviewer: How do you think this style has changed since *On the Road*?
Kerouac: What style? Oh, the style of *On the Road*. Well as I say, Cowley riddled the original style of the manuscript there, without my power to complain, and since then my books are all published as written, as I say, and the style has varied from the highly experimental speedwriting of *Railroad Earth* to the ingrown toenail packed mystical style of *Tristessa,* the *Notes-from-the-Underground* (by Dostoevsky) confessional madness of *The Subterraneans,* the perfection of the three as one in *Big Sur,* I'd say, which tells a plain tale in a smooth buttery literate run, to *Satori in Paris* which is really the first book I wrote with drink at my side (cognac and malt liquor) . . . and not to overlook *Book of Dreams,* the style of a person half awake from sleep and ripping it out in pencil by the bed . . . yes, pencil . . . what a job! Bleary eyes, insaned mind bemused and mystified by sleep, details that pop out even as you write them you don't know what they mean, till you wake up, have coffee, look at it, and see the logic of dreams in dream language itself, see? . . . and finally I decided in my tired middle age to slow down and did *Vanity of Duluoz* in a more moderate style so that, having been so esoteric all these years, some earlier readers would come back and see what ten years had done to my life and thinking . . . which is after all the only thing I've got to offer, the true story of what I saw and how I saw it.

Interviewer: You dictated sections of *Visions of Cody.* Have you used this method since?
Kerouac: I didn't dictate sections of *Visions of Cody.* I typed up a segment of taped conversation with Neal Cassady, or Cody, talking about his early adventures in L.A. It's four chapters. I haven't used this method since; it really doesn't come out right, well, with Neal and with myself, when all written down and with all the Ahs and the Ohs and the Ahums and the fearful fact that the damn thing is turning and you're *forced* not to waste electricity or tape. . . . Then again, I don't know, I might have to resort to that eventually; I'm getting tired and going blind. This question stumps me. At any rate, everybody's

doing it, I hear, but I'm still scribbling. . . . McLuhan says we're getting more oral so I guess we'll all learn to talk into the machine better and better.

Interviewer: What is that state of "Yeatsian semi-trance" which provides the ideal atmosphere for spontaneous writing?
Kerouac: Well, there it is, how can you be in a trance with your mouth yapping away . . . writing at least is a silent meditation even though you're going a hundred miles an hour. Remember that scene in *La Dolce Vita* where the old priest is mad because a mob of maniacs have shown up to see the tree where the kids saw the Virgin Mary? He says, "Visions are not available in all this frenetic foolishness and yelling and pushing; visions are only obtainable in silence and meditation." Thar. Yup.

Interviewer: You have said that haiku is not written spontaneously but is reworked and revised. Is this true of all your poetry? Why must the method for writing poetry differ from that of prose?
Kerouac: No, first; haiku is best reworked and revised. I know, I tried. It has to be completely economical, no foliage and flowers and language rhythm, it has to be a simple little picture in three little lines. At least that's the way the old masters did it, spending months on three little lines and coming up, say, with:

> In the abandoned boat,
> The hail
> Bounces about.

That's Shiki.

But as for my regular English verse, I knocked it off fast like the prose, using, get this, the size of the notebook page for the form and length of the poem, just as a musician has to get out, a jazz musician, his statement within a certain number of bars, within one chorus, which spills over into the next, but he has to stop where the chorus page *stops*. And finally, too, in poetry you can be completely free to say anything you want, you don't have to tell a story, you can use secret puns, that's why I always say, when writing prose, "No time for poetry now, get your plain tale." (*Drinks are served*)

Interviewer: How do you write haiku?
Kerouac: Haiku? You want to hear Haiku? You see you got to compress into three short lines a great big story. First you start with a haiku situation—so

you see a leaf, as I told her the other night, falling on the back of a sparrow during a great big October wind storm. A big leaf falls on the back of a little sparrow. How you going to compress that into three lines? Now in Japanese you got to compress it into seventeen syllables. We don't have to do that in American—or English—because we don't have the same syllabic bullshit that your Japanese language has. So you say: Little sparrow—you don't have to say little—everybody knows a sparrow is little . . . because they fall . . . so you say

Sparrow
with big leaf on its back—
Windstorm

No good, don't work, I reject it.

A little sparrow
when an Autumn leaf suddenly sticks to its back
from the wind.

Hah, that does it. No, it's a little bit too long. See? It's already a little bit too long, Berrigan, you know what I mean?

Interviewer: Seems like there's an extra word or something, like "when." How about leaving out "when?" Say:

A sparrow
an autumn leaf suddenly sticks to its back—
From the wind!

Kerouac: Hey, that's all right. I think "when" was the extra word. You got the right idea there, O'Hara! A sparrow, an autumn leaf suddenly—we don't have to say "suddenly" do we?

A sparrow
an autumn leaf sticks to its back—
From the wind!

(Kerouac writes final version into spiral notebook)

Interviewer: "Suddenly" is absolutely the kind of word we don't need there. When you publish that will you give me a footnote saying you asked me a couple of questions?
Kerouac: (*Writes*) Berrigan noticed. Right?

Interviewer: Do you write poetry very much? Do you write other poetry besides haiku?
Kerouac: It's hard to write Haiku. I write long silly Indian poems. You want to hear my long silly Indian Poem?

Interviewer: What kind of Indian?
Kerouac: Iroquois. As you know from looking at me. (*Reads from notebook*)

> On the lawn on the way to the store
> 44 years old for the neighbors to hear
> hey, looka, Ma I hurt myself. Especially
> with that squirt.

What's that mean?

Interviewer: Say it again.
Kerouac: Hey, looka, Ma, I hurt myself, while on the way to the store I hurt myself I fell on the lawn I yell to my mother hey looka, Ma, I hurt myself. I add, especially with that squirt.

Interviewer: You fell over a sprinkler?
Kerouac: No, my father's squirt into my Ma.

Interviewer: From that distance?
Kerouac: Oh, I quit. No, I know you wouldn't get that one. I had to explain it. (*Opens notebook again and reads*)

> Goy means Joy.

Interviewer: Send that one to Ginsberg.
Kerouac: (*Reads*) Happy people so called are hypocrites—it means the happiness wavelength can't work without necessary deceit, without certain scheming and lies and hiding. Hypocrisy and deceit, no Indians. No smiling.

Interviewer: No Indians?

Kerouac: The reason you really have a hidden hostility towards me, Berrigan, is because of the French and Indian War.

Interviewer: That could be.

Saroyan: I saw a football picture of you in the cellar of Horace Mann. You were pretty fat in those days.

Stella: Tuffy! Here Tuffy! Come on kitty . . .

Kerouac: Stella, let's have another bottle or two. Yeah, I'm going to murder everybody if they let me go. I did. Hot fudge sundaes! Boom! I used to have two or three hot fudge sundaes before every game. Lou Little . . .

Interviewer: He was your coach at Columbia?

Kerouac: Lou Little was my coach at Columbia. My father went up to him and said you sneaky long-nosed finagler. . . . He says why don't you let my son, Ti Jean, Jack, start in the Army game so he can get back at his great enemy from Lowell? And Lou Little says because he's not ready. Who says he's not ready? I say he's not ready. My father says why you long nose banana nose big crook, get out of my sight! And he comes stomping out of the office smoking a big cigar. Come out of here Jack, let's get out of here. So we left Columbia together. And also when I was in the United States Navy during the war—1942—right in front of the Admirals, he walked in and says Jack, you are right! The Germans should not be our enemies. They should be our allies, as it will be proven in time. And the Admirals were all there with their mouths open, and my father would take no shit from nobody—my father didn't have nothing but a big belly about this big (*gestures with arms out in front of him*) and he would go POOM! (*Kerouac gets up and demonstrates, by puffing his belly out in front of him with explosive force and saying POOM!*) One time he was walking down the street with my mother, arm in arm, down the lower East Side. In the old days, you know, the 1940s. And here comes a whole bunch of rabbis walking arm in arm . . . tee-dah teedah-teedah . . . and they wouldn't part for this Christian man and his wife. So my father went POOM! and he knocked a rabbi right in the gutter. Then he took my mother and walked on through.

Now, if you don't like that, Berrigan, that's the history of my family. They don't take no shit from nobody. In due time I ain't going to take no shit from nobody. You can record that.

Is this my wine?

Interviewer: Was *The Town and the City* written under spontaneous composition principles?

Kerouac: Some of it, sire. I also wrote another version that's hidden under the floorboards, with Burroughs.

Interviewer: Yes, I've heard rumors of that book. Everybody wants to get at that book.

Kerouac: It's called *And the Hippos Were Boiled in Their Tanks.* The hippos. Because Burroughs and I were sitting in a bar one night and we heard a newscaster saying . . . "and so the Egyptians attacked blah blah . . . and meanwhile there was a great fire in the zoo in London and the fire raced across the fields and the hippos were boiled in their tanks! Goodnight everyone!" That's Bill, he noticed that. Because he notices them kind of things.

Interviewer: You really did type up his *Naked Lunch* manuscript for him in Tangiers?

Kerouac: No . . . the first part. The first two chapters. I went to bed, and I had nightmares . . . of great long balonies coming out of my mouth. I had nightmares typing up that manuscript . . . I said, "Bill!" He said, "Keep typing it." He said, "I bought you a goddamn kerosene stove here in North Africa, you know." Among the Arabs . . . it's hard to get a kerosene stove. I'd light up the kerosene stove and take some bedding and a little pot, or kif as we called it there . . . or maybe sometimes hasheesh . . . there by the way it's legal . . . and I'd go toktoktoktoktoktok and when I went to bed at night, these things kept coming out of my mouth. So finally these other guys showed up like Alan Ansen and Allen Ginsberg, and they spoiled the whole manuscript because they didn't type it up the way he wrote it.

Interviewer: Grove Press has been issuing his Olympia Press books with lots of changes and things added.

Kerouac: Well, in my opinion Burroughs hasn't given us anything that would interest our breaking hearts since he wrote like he did in *Naked Lunch*. Now all he does is that break-up stuff it's called . . . where you write a page of prose, you write another page of prose . . . then you fold it over and you cut it up and you put it together . . . and shit like that . . .

Interviewer: What about *Junkie*, though?

Kerouac: It's a classic. It's better than Hemingway—it's just like Hemingway but even a little better too. It says: Danny comes into my pad one night and says, Hey, Bill, can I borrow your sap. Your sap—do you know what a sap is?

Saroyan: A blackjack?

Kerouac: It's a blackjack. Bill says, I pulled out my underneath drawer, and underneath some nice shirts I pulled out my blackjack. I gave it to Danny and said, Now don't lose it Danny—Danny says, Don't worry I won't lose it. He goes off and loses it.

Sap . . . blackjack . . . that's me. Sap . . . blackjack.

Interviewer: That's a Haiku: sap, blackjack, that's me. You better write that down.

Kerouac: No.

Interviewer: Maybe I'll write that down. Do you mind if I use that one?

Kerouac: Up your ass with Mobil gas!

Interviewer: You don't believe in collaborations? Have you ever done any collaborations, other than with publishers?

Kerouac: I did a couple of collaborations in bed with Bill Cannastra in lofts. With blondes.

Interviewer: Was he the guy that tried to climb off the subway train at Astor Place, in Holmes's *Go*?

Kerouac: Yes. Yeah, well he says let's take all our clothes off and run around the block . . . it was raining you know. Sixteenth Street off Seventh Avenue. I said, well, I'll keep my shorts on— he says no, no shorts. I said I'm going to keep my shorts on. He said all right, but I'm not going to wear mine. And we trot trottrot trot down the block. Sixteenth to Seventeenth . . . and we come back and run up the stairs—nobody saw us.

Interviewer: What time of day?

Kerouac: But he was absolutely naked . . . about 3 or 4 A.M. It rained. And everybody was there. He was dancing on broken glass and playing Bach. Bill was the guy who used to teeter off his roof—six flights up you know? He'd go—"you want me to fall?"—we'd say no, Bill, no. He was an Italian. Italians are wild you know.

Interviewer: Did he write? What did he do?
Kerouac: He says, "Jack, come with me and look down through this peephole." We looked down through the peephole, we saw a lot of things . . . into his toilet.

I said, "I'm not interested in that, Bill." He said, "You're not interested in anything." Auden would come the next day, the next afternoon, for cocktails. Maybe with Chester Kallman. Tennessee Williams.

Interviewer: Was Neal Cassady around in those days? Did you already know Neal Cassady when you were involved with Bill Cannastra?
Kerouac: Oh yes, yes, ahem . . . he had a great big pack of pot. He always was a pot happy man.

Interviewer: Why do you think Neal doesn't write?
Kerouac: He has written . . . beautifully! He has written better than I have. Neal's a very funny guy. He's a real Californian. We had more fun than five thousand Socony Gasoline Station attendants can have. In my opinion he's the most intelligent man I've ever met in my life. Neal Cassady. He's a Jesuit by the way. He used to sing in the choir. He was a choir boy in the Catholic churches of Denver. And he taught me everything that I now do believe about anything that there may be to be believed about divinity.

Interviewer: About Edgar Cayce?
Kerouac: No, before he found out about Edgar Cayce he told me all these things in the section of the life he led when he was on the road with me—he said, We know God, don't we, Jack? I said, Yessir boy. He said, Don't we know that nothing's going to happen wrong? Yessir. And we're going to go on and on . . . and hmmmmm ja-bmmmmmmm. . . . He was perfect. And he's always perfect. Everytime he comes to see me I can't get a word in edgewise.

Interviewer: You wrote about Neal playing football, in *Visions of Cody.*
Kerouac: Yes, he was a very good football player. He picked up two beatniks that time in blue jeans in North Beach Frisco. He said I got to go, bang bang, do I got to go? He's working on the railroad . . . had his watch out . . . 2:15,

boy I got to be there by 2:20. I tell you boys drive me over down there so I be on time with my train . . . So I can get my train on down to—what's the name of that place—San Jose? They say sure kid and Neal says here's the pot. So—"We maybe look like great bleat beatniks with great beards . . . but we are cops. And we are arresting you."

So, a guy went to the jailhouse and interviewed him from the *New York Post* and he said tell that Kerouac if he still believes in me to send me a typewriter. So I sent Allen Ginsberg one hundred dollars to get a typewriter for Neal. And Neal got the typewriter. And he wrote notes on it, but they wouldn't let him take the notes out. I don't know where the typewriter is. Genet wrote all of *Our Lady of the Flowers* in the shithouse . . . the jailhouse. There's a great writer, Jean Genet. He kept writing and kept writing until he got to a point where he was going to come by writing about it . . . until he came into his bed—in the can. The French can. The French jail. Prison. And that was the end of the chapter. Every chapter is Genet coming off. Which I must admit Sartre noticed.

Interviewer: You think that's a different kind of spontaneous writing?
Kerouac: Well, I could go to jail and I could write every night a chapter about Magee, Magoo, and Molly. It's beautiful. Genet is really *the* most honest writer we've had since Kerouac and Burroughs. But he came before us. He's older. Well, he's the same age as Burroughs. But I don't think I've been dishonest. Man, I've had a good time! God, man, I rode around this country free as a bee. But Genet is a very tragic and beautiful writer. And I give them the crown. And the laurel wreath. I don't give the laurel wreath to Richard Wilbur! *Or* Robert Lowell. Give it to Jean Genet and William Seward Burroughs. *And* to Allen Ginsberg and to Gregory Corso, especially.

Interviewer: Jack, how about Peter Orlovsky's writings. Do you like Peter's things?
Kerouac: Peter Orlovsky is an idiot!! He's a Russian idiot. Not even Russian, he's Polish.

Interviewer: He's written some fine poems.
Kerouac: Oh yeah. My . . . what poems?

Interviewer: He has a beautiful poem called "Second Poem."
Kerouac: "My brother pisses in the bed . . . and I go in the subway and I see two people kissing . . ."

Interviewer: No, the poem that says "it's more creative to paint the floor than to sweep it."

Kerouac: That's a lot of shit! That is the kind of poetry that was written by another Polish idiot who was a Polish nut called Apollinaire. Apollinaire is not his real name, you know.

There are some fellows in San Francisco that told me that Peter was an idiot. But I like idiots, and I enjoy his poetry. Think about that, Berrigan. But for my taste, it's Gregory.

Give me one of those.

Interviewer: One of these pills?

Kerouac: Yeah. What are they? Forked clarinets?

Interviewer: They're called Obetrol. Neal is the one that told me about them.

Kerouac: Overtones?

Interviewer: Overtones? No, overcoats.

Saroyan: What was that you said . . . at the back of the Grove anthology . . . that you let the line go a little longer to fill it up with secret images that come at the end of the sentence.

Kerouac: He's a real Armenian! Sediment. Delta. Mud. It's where you start a poem . . .

> As I was walking down the street one day
> I saw a lake where people were cutting off my rear,
> 17,000 priests singing like George Burns

and then you go on . . .

> And I'm making jokes about me
> and breaking my bones in the earth
> and here I am the great John Armenian
> coming back to earth

now you remember where you were in the beginning and you say . . .

> Ahaha! Tatatatadooda . . . Screw Turkey!

See? You remembered the line at the end . . . you lose your mind in the middle.
Saroyan: Right.
Kerouac: That applies to prose as well as poetry.

Interviewer: But in prose you are telling a story . . .
Kerouac: In prose you make the paragraph. Every paragraph is a poem.

Interviewer: Is that how you write a paragraph?
Kerouac: When I was running downtown there, and I was going to do this, and I was laying there, with that girl there, and a guy took out his scissors and I took him inside there, he showed me some dirty pictures. And I went out and fell downstairs with the potato bags.

Interviewer: Did you ever like Gertrude Stein's work?
Kerouac: Never interested me too much. I liked *Melanctha* a little bit.
I should really go to school and teach these kids. I could make two thousand bucks a week. You can't learn these things. You know why? Because you have to be born with tragic fathers.

Interviewer: You can only do that if you are born in New England.
Kerouac: Incidentally, my father said your father wasn't tragic.
Saroyan: I don't think my father is tragic.
Kerouac: My father said that Saroyan . . . William Saroyan ain't tragic at all . . . he's fulla shit. And I had a big argument with him. *The Daring Young Man on the Flying Trapeze* is pretty tragic, I would say.
Saroyan: He was just a young man then, you know.
Kerouac: Yeah, but he was hungry, and he was on Times Square. Flying. A young man on the flying trapeze. That was a beautiful story. It killed me when I was a kid.

Interviewer: Do you remember a story by William Saroyan about the Indian who came to town and bought a car and got the little kid to drive it for him?
Stella: A Cadillac.
Kerouac: What town was that?
Saroyan: Fresno. That was Fresno.
Kerouac: Well, you remember the night I was taking a big nap and you came up outside my window on a white horse . . .

Saroyan: *The Summer of the Beautiful White Horse.*
Kerouac: And I looked out the window and said what is this? You said, "My name is Aram. And I'm on a white horse."
Saroyan: Moorad.
Kerouac: My name is Moorad, excuse me. No, my name is . . . I was Aram, you were Moorad. You said, "Wake up!" I didn't want to wake up. I wanted to sleep. *My Name Is Aram* is the name of the book. You stole a white horse from a farmer and you woke up me, Aram, to go riding with you.
Saroyan: Moorad was the crazy one who stole the horse.
Kerouac: Hey, what's that you gave me there?

Interviewer: Obetrol.
Kerouac: Oh, obies.

Interviewer: What about jazz and bop as influences rather than . . . Saroyan, Hemingway and Wolfe?
Kerouac: Yes, jazz and bop, in the sense of a, say, a tenor man drawing a breath and blowing a phrase on his saxophone, till he runs out of breath, and when he does, his sentence, his statement's been made . . . that's how I therefore separate my sentences, as breath separations of the mind . . . I formulated the theory of breath as measure, in prose and verse, never mind what Olson, Charles Olson says, I formulated that theory in 1953 at the request of Burroughs and Ginsberg. Then there's the raciness and freedom and humor of jazz instead of all that dreary analysis and things like "James entered the room, and lit a cigarette. He thought Jane might have thought this too vague a gesture . . ." You know the stuff. As for Saroyan, yes I loved him as a teenager, he really got me out of the nineteenth century rut I was trying to study, not only his funny tone but his neat Armenian poetic I don't know what . . . he just got me . . . Hemingway was fascinating, the pearls of words on a white page giving you an exact picture . . . but Wolfe was a torrent of American heaven and hell that opened my eyes to America as a subject in itself.

Interviewer: How about the movies?
Kerouac: Yes, we've all been influenced by movies. Malcolm Cowley incidentally mentioned this many times. He's very perceptive sometimes: he mentioned that *Doctor Sax* continually mentions urine, and quite naturally it

does because I had no other place to write it but on a closed toilet seat in a little tile toilet in Mexico City so as to get away from the guests inside the apartment. There incidentally is a style truly hallucinated as I wrote it all on pot. No pun intended. Ho ho.

Interviewer: How has Zen influenced your work?

Kerouac: What's really influenced my work is the Mahayana Buddhism, the original Buddhism of Gotama Sakyamuni, the Buddha himself, of the India of old . . . Zen is what's left of his Buddhism, or Bodhi, after its passing into China and then into Japan. The part of Zen that's influenced my writing is the Zen contained in the haiku, like I said, the three line, seventeen syllable poems written hundreds of years ago by guys like Basho, Issa, Shiki, and there've been recent masters. A sentence that's short and sweet with a sudden jump of thought in it is a kind of haiku, and there's a lot of freedom and fun in surprising yourself with that, let the mind willy-nilly jump from the branch to the bird. But my serious Buddhism, that of ancient India, has influenced that part in my writing that you might call religious, or fervent, or pious, almost as much as Catholicism has. Original Buddhism referred to continual conscious compassion, brotherhood, the *dana paramita* meaning the perfection of charity, don't step on the bug, all that, humility, mendicancy, the sweet sorrowful face of the Buddha (who was of Aryan origin by the way, I mean of Persian warrior caste, and not Oriental as pictured) . . . in original Buddhism no young kid coming to a monastery was warned that "here we bury them alive." He was simply given soft encouragement to meditate and be kind. The beginning of Zen was when Buddha, however, assembled all the monks together to announce a sermon and choose the first patriarch of the Mahayana church: instead of speaking, he simply held up a flower. Everybody was flabbergasted except Kasyapa, who smiled. Kasyapa was appointed the first patriarch. This idea appealed to the Chinese like the Sixth Patriarch Hui-Neng who said, "From the beginning nothing ever was" and wanted to tear up the records of Buddha's sayings as kept in the sutras; sutras are "threads of discourse." In a way, then, Zen is a gentle but goofy form of heresy, though there must be some real kindly old monks somewhere and we've heard about the nutty ones. I haven't been to Japan. Your Maha roshi yoshi is simply a disciple of all this and not the founder of anything new at all, of course. On the Johnny Carson show he didn't even mention Buddha's name. Maybe his Buddha is Mia.

Interviewer: How come you've never written about Jesus? You've written about Buddha. Wasn't Jesus a great guy too?
Kerouac: I've never written about Jesus? In other words, you're an insane phoney who comes to my house . . . and . . . all I *write about* is Jesus. I am Everhard Mercurian, General of the Jesuit Army.

Saroyan: What's the difference between Jesus and Buddha?
Kerouac: That's a very good question. There is no difference.

Saroyan: No difference?
Kerouac: But there is a difference between the original Buddha of India, and the Buddha of Vietnam who just shaves his hair and puts on a yellow robe and is a Communist agitating agent. The original Buddha wouldn't even walk on young grass so that he wouldn't destroy it. He was born in Gorakpur, the son of the Consul of the invading Persian hordes. And he was called Sage of the Warriors, and he had 17,000 broads dancing for him all night, holding out flowers, saying you want to smell it, my Lord? He says git outta here you whore. He laid a lot of them you know. But by the time he was thirty-one years old he got sick and tired . . . his father was protecting him from what was going on outside the town. And so he went out on a horse, against his father's orders and he saw a woman dying—a man being burnt on a ghat. And he said, What is all this death and decay? The servant said that is the way things go on. Your father was hiding you from the way things go on.

He says, What? My father!!—Get my horse, saddle my horse! Ride me into the forest! They ride into the forest; he says, Now take the saddle off the horse. Put it on your horse, hang it on . . . take my horse by the rein and ride back to the castle and tell my father I'll never see him again! And the servant, Kandaka, cried, he said, I'll never see you again. I don't care! Go on! Shoosh! Get away!!

He spent seven years in the forest. Biting his teeth together. Nothing happened. Tormenting himself with starvation. He said, I will keep my teeth bit together until I find the cause of death. Then one day he was stumbling across the Rapti river, and he fainted in the river. And a young girl came by with a bowl of milk and said, My lord, a bowl of milk. (*Slurpppp*) He said, That gives me great energy, thank you my dear. Then he went and sat under the Bo tree. Figuerosa. The fig tree. He said, Now . . . (*Demonstrates posture*) . . . I will cross my legs . . . and grit my teeth until I find the cause of death. Two o'clock in the

morning, a hundred thousand phantoms assailed him. He didn't move. Three
o'clock in the morning, the great blue ghosts!! Arrghhh!!! All *accosted* him.
(You see I am really Scottish.) Four o'clock in the morning the mad maniacs
of hell . . . came out of manhole covers . . . in New York City. You know Wall
Street where the steam comes out? You know Wall Street, where the manhole
covers . . . steam comes up? You take off them covers—yaaaaaahhh!!!!! Six
o'clock, everything was peaceful—the birds started to trill, and he said,
"Aha! . . . the cause of death . . . the cause of death is birth."

Simple? So he started walking down the road to Benares in India . . . with
long hair, like you, see.

So, three guys. One says hey, here comes Buddha there who uh starved
with us in the forest. When he sits down here on that bucket, don't wash his
feet. So Buddha sits down on the bucket . . . the guy rushes up and washes his
feet. Why dost thou wash his feet? Buddha says, "Because I go to Benares to
beat the drum of life." And what is that? "That the cause of death is birth."
"What do you mean?" "I'll show you."

A woman comes up with a dead baby in her arms. Says, Bring my child
back to life if you are the Lord. He says, Sure I'll do that anytime. Just go and
find one family in Sravasti that ain't had a death in the last five years. Get a
mustard seed from them and bring it to me. And I'll bring your child back to
life. She went all over town, man, two million people, Sravasti the town was, a
bigger town than Benares by the way, and she came back and said, I can't find
no such family. They've all had deaths within five years. He said, "Then, bury
your baby."

Then, his jealous cousin, Devadatta, (that's Ginsberg you see . . . I am
Buddha and Ginsberg is Devadatta) gets this elephant drunk . . . great big bull
elephant drunk on whiskey. The elephant goes up!!!! (*Trumpets like elephant
going up*)—with a big trunk, and Buddha comes up in the road and gets the
elephant and goes like this (*Kneels*). And the elephant kneels down. "You are
buried in sorrow's mud! Quiet your trunk! Stay there!" . . . He's an elephant
trainer. Then Devadatta rolled a big boulder over a cliff. And it almost hit
Buddha's head. Just missed. Boooom! He says, That's Devadatta again. Then
Buddha went like this (*Paces back and forth*) in front of his boys, you see.
Behind him was his cousin that loved him . . . Ananda . . . which means love in
Sanskrit. (*Keeps pacing*) This is what you do in jail to keep in shape.

I know a lot of stories about Buddha, but I don't know exactly what he
said every time. But I know what he said about the guy who spit at him. He

said, "Since I can't use your abuse you may have it back." He was great.
(*Kerouac plays piano. Drinks are served.*)
Saroyan: There's something there.

Interviewer: My mother used to play that. I'm not sure how we can transcribe those notes onto a page. We may have to include a record of you playing the piano. Will you play that piece again for the record, Mr. Paderewski? Can you play "Alouette"?
Kerouac: No. Only Afro-Germanic music. After all, I'm a square head. I wonder what whiskey will do to those obies.

Interviewer: What about ritual and superstition? Do you have any about yourself when you get down to work?
Kerouac: I had a ritual once of lighting a candle and writing by its light and blowing it out when I was done for the night . . . also kneeling and praying before starting (I got that from a French movie about George Frederick Handel) . . . but now I simply hate to write. My superstition? I'm beginning to suspect that full moon. Also I'm hung up on the number 9 though I'm told a Piscean like myself should stick to number 7; but I try to do 9 touchdowns a day, that is, I stand on my head in the bathroom, on a slipper, and touch the floor 9 times with my toe tips, while balanced. This is incidentally more than Yoga, it's an athletic feat, I mean imagine calling me "unbalanced" after that. Frankly I do feel that my mind is going. So another "ritual" as you call it, is to pray to Jesus to preserve my sanity and my energy so I can help my family: that being my paralyzed mother, and my wife, and the ever-present kitties. Okay?

Interviewer: You typed out *On the Road* in three weeks, *The Subterraneans* . . . in three days and nights. Do you still produce at this fantastic rate? Can you say something of the genesis of a work before you sit down and begin that terrific typing—how much of it is set in your mind, for example?
Kerouac: You think out what actually happened, you tell friends long stories about it, you mull it over in your mind, you connect it together at leisure, then when the time comes to pay the rent again you force yourself to sit at the typewriter, or at the writing notebook, and get it over with as fast as you can . . . and there's no harm in that because you've got the whole story lined up. Now how that's done depends on what kind of steeltrap you've got up in that little old head. This sounds boastful but a girl once told me I had a steeltrap

brain, meaning I'd catch her with a statement she'd made an hour ago
even though our talk had rambled a million lightyears away from that
point . . . you know what I mean, like a lawyer's mind, say. All of it is in my
mind, naturally, except that language that is used at the time that it is used. . . .
And as for *On the Road* and *The Subterraneans*, no I can't write that fast any
more. . . . Writing the Subs in three nights was really a fantastic athletic feat as
well as mental, you shoulda seen me after I was done . . . I was pale as a sheet
and had lost fifteen pounds and looked strange in the mirror. What I do now is
write something like an average of 8,000 words a sitting, in the middle of the
night, and another about a week later, resting and sighing in between. I really
hate to write. I get no fun out of it because I can't get up and say I'm working,
close my door, have coffee brought to me, and sit there camping like a "man of
letters" "doing his eight hour day of work" and thereby incidentally filling the
printing world with a lot of dreary self-imposed cant and bombast . . . bombast
is Scottish word for stuffing for a pillow. Haven't you heard a politician use
1500 words to say something he could have said in exactly three words? So
I get it out of the way so as not to bore myself either.
Saroyan: Do you usually try to see everything clearly and not think of any
words—just to see everything as clear as possible and then write out of the
feeling. With *Tristessa*, for example.
Kerouac: You sound like a writing seminar at Indiana University.
Saroyan: I know but . . .
Kerouac: All I did was suffer with that poor girl and then when she fell on
her head and almost killed herself . . . remember when she fell on her
head? . . . and she was all busted up and everything. She was the most
gorgeous little Indian chick you ever saw. I say Indian, pure Indian.
Esperanza Villanueva. Villanueva is a Spanish name from I don't know
where—Castile. But she's Indian. So she's half Indian, half Spanish . . .
beauty. Absolute beauty. She had bones, man, just bones, skin and bones.
And I didn't write in the book how I finally nailed her. You know? I did. I
finally nailed her. She said, "Shhhhhhhhhh! Don't let the landlord hear." She
said, "Remember, I'm very weak and sick." I said, "I know, I've been writing a
book about how you're weak and sick."

Interviewer: How come you didn't put that part in the book?
Kerouac: Because Claude's wife told me not to put it in. She said it would
spoil the book.

But it was not a conquest. She was out like a light. On M. M., that's Morphine. And in fact I made a big run for her from way uptown to downtown to the slum district . . . and I said, here's your stuff. She said, "Shhhhhh!" She gave herself a shot . . . and I said, Ah . . . now's the time. And I got my little nogood piece. But . . . it was certainly justification of Mexico!
Stella: Here kitty! He's gone out again.
Kerouac: She was nice, you would have liked her. Her real name was Esperanza. You know what that means?

Interviewer: No.
Kerouac: In Spanish, hope. Tristessa means in Spanish, sadness, but her real name was Hope. And she's now married to the police chief of Mexico City.
Stella: Not quite.
Kerouac: Well, you're not Esperanza—I'll tell you that.
Stella: No, I know that, dear.
Kerouac: She was the skinniest . . . and shy . . . as a rail.
Stella: She's married to one of the lieutenants, you told me, not to the chief.
Kerouac: She's all right. One of these days I'm going to go see her again.
Stella: Over my dead body.

Interviewer: Were you really writing *Tristessa* while you were there in Mexico? You didn't write it later?
Kerouac: First part written in Mexico, second part written in . . . Mexico. That's right. 'Fifty-five first part', Fifty-six second part. What's the importance about that? I'm not Charles Olson, the great artist!

Interviewer: We're just getting the facts.
Kerouac: Charles Olson gives you all the dates. You know. Everything about how he found the hound dog on the beach in Gloucester. Found somebody jacking-off on the beach at . . . what do they call it? Vancouver Beach? Dig Dog River? . . . Dogtown. That's what they call it, "Dogtown." Well this is Shit-town on the Merrimac. Lowell is called Shit-town on the Merrimac. I'm not going to write a poem called Shit-town and insult my town. But if I was six foot six I could write anything, couldn't I?

Interviewer: How do you get along now with other writers? Do you correspond with them?

Kerouac: I correspond with John Clellon Holmes but less and less each year, I'm getting lazy. I can't answer my fan mail because I haven't got a secretary to take dictation, do the typing, get the stamps, envelopes, all that . . . and I have nothing to answer. I ain't gonna spend the rest of my life smiling and shaking hands and sending and receiving platitudes, like a candidate for political office, because I'm a writer—I've got to let my mind alone, like Greta Garbo. Yet when I go out, or receive sudden guests, we all have more fun than a barrel of monkeys.

Interviewer: What are the work-destroyers?
Kerouac: Work-destroyers . . . work-destroyers. Time-killers? I'd say mainly the attentions which are tendered to a writer of "notoriety" (notice I don't say "fame") by secretly ambitious would-be writers, who come around, or write, or call, for the sake of the services which are properly the services of a bloody literary agent. When I was an unknown struggling young writer, as saying goes, I did my own footwork, I hotfooted up and down Madison Avenue for years, publisher to publisher, agent to agent, and never once in my life wrote a letter to a published famous author asking for advice, or help, or, in Heaven above, have the nerve to actually *mail* my manuscripts to some poor author who then has to hustle to mail it back before he's accused of stealing my ideas. My advice to young writers is to get themselves an agent on their own, maybe through their college professors (as I got my first publishers through my prof Mark Van Doren) and do their own footwork, or "thing" as the slang goes . . . So the work-destroyers are nothing but certain *people.*

The work-preservers are the solitudes of night, "when the whole wide world is fast asleep."

Interviewer: What do you find the best time and place for writing?
Kerouac: The desk in the room, near the bed, with a good light, midnight till dawn, a drink when you get tired, preferably at home, but if you have no home, make a home out of your hotel room or motel room or pad: peace. (*Picks up harmonica and plays*) Boy, can I play!

Interviewer: What about writing under the influence of drugs?
Kerouac: Poem 230 from *Mexico City Blues* is a poem written purely on morphine. Every line in this poem was written within an hour of one another . . . high on a big dose of M. (*Finds volume and reads*)

Love's multitudinous boneyard of decay
An hour later:
The spilled milk of heroes
An hour later:
Destruction of silk kerchiefs by dust storm,
An hour later:
Caress of heroes blindfolded to posts,
An hour later:
Murder victims admitted to this life,
An hour later:
Skeletons bartering fingers and joints,
An hour later:
The quivering meat of the elephants of kindness being torn apart by vultures
(See where Ginsberg stole that from me?)
An hour later: Conceptions of delicate kneecaps.
Say that, Saroyan.

Saroyan: Conceptions of delicate kneecaps.
Kerouac: Very good. Fear of rats dripping with bacteria. An hour later:
Golgotha Cold Hope for Gold Hope. Say that.
Saroyan: Golgotha Cold Hope for Cold Hope.
Kerouac: That's pretty cold.
An hour later: Damp leaves of Autumn against the wood of boats,
An hour later: Seahorse's delicate imagery of glue . . .
Ever see a little seahorse in the ocean? They're built of glue . . . did you ever
sniff a seahorse? No, say that.
Saroyan: Seahorse's delicate imagery of glue.
Kerouac: You'll do, Saroyan. Death by long exposure to defilement.
Saroyan: Death by long exposure to defilement.
Kerouac: Frightening ravishing mysterious beings concealing their sex.
Saroyan: Frightening ravishing mysterious beings concealing their sex.
Kerouac: Pieces of the Buddha-material frozen and sliced microscopically
In Morgues of the North.
Saroyan: Hey, I can't say that. Pieces of the Buddha-material frozen and
sliced microscopically in Morgues of the North.
Kerouac: Penis apples going to seed.
Saroyan: Penis apples going to seed.

Kerouac: The severed gullets more numerous than sands.
Saroyan: The severed gullets more numerous than sands.
Kerouac: Like kissing my kitten in the belly.
Saroyan: Like kissing my kitten in the belly.
Kerouac: The softness of our reward.
Saroyan: The softness of our reward.
Kerouac: Is he really William Saroyan's son? That's wonderful! Would you mind repeating that?

Interviewer: We should be asking you a lot of very straight serious questions. When did you meet Allen Ginsberg?
Kerouac: First I met Claude.* And then I met Allen and then I met Burroughs. Claude came in through the fire escape . . . there were gunshots down in the alley—Pow! Pow! and it was raining, and my wife says, here comes Claude. And here comes this blond guy through the fire escape, all wet. I said, "What's this all about, what the hell is this?" He says, "They're chasing me." Next day in walks Allen Ginsberg carrying books. Sixteen years old with his ears sticking out. He says, "Well, discretion is the better part of valor!" I said, "Aw shutup. You little twitch." Then the next day here comes Burroughs wearing a seersucker suit, followed by the other guy.

Interviewer: What other guy?
Kerouac: It was the guy who wound up in the river. This was this guy from New Orleans that Claude killed and threw in the river. Stabbed him twelve times in the heart with a Boy Scout knife.

When Claude was fourteen he was the most beautiful blond boy in New Orleans. And he joined the Boy Scout troop . . . and the Boy Scout Master was a big redheaded fairy who went to school at St. Louis University, I think it was.

And he had already been in love with a guy who looked just like Claude in Paris. And this guy chased Claude all over the country; this guy had him thrown out of Baldwin, Tulane, and Andover Prep. . . . It's a queer tale, but Claude isn't a queer.

Interviewer: What about the influence of Ginsberg and Burroughs? Did you ever have any sense then of the mark the three of you would have on American writing?

---

*"Claude," a pseudonym, is also used in *Vanity of Duluoz*.

Kerouac: I was determined to be a "great writer," in quotes, like Thomas
Wolfe, see . . . Allen was always reading and writing poetry . . . Burroughs read
a lot and walked around looking at things. . . . The influence we exerted on
one another has been written about over and over again . . . We were just three
interested characters, in the interesting big city of New York, around cam-
puses, libraries, cafeterias. A lot of the details you'll find in *Vanity* . . . in *On the
Road* where Burroughs is Bull Lee and Ginsberg is Carlo Marx . . . in
Subterraneans, where they're Frank Carmody and Adam Moorad respectively,
elsewhere. In other words, though I don't want to be rude to you for this
honor, I am so busy interviewing myself in my novels, and have been so busy
writing down these self-interviews, that I don't see why I should draw breath
in pain every year of the last ten years to repeat and repeat to everybody who
interviews me what I've already explained in the books themselves. . . .
(Hundreds of journalists, thousands of students.) It beggars sense. And it's not
that important. It's our work that counts, if anything at all, and I'm not proud
of mine or theirs or anybody's since Thoreau and others like that, maybe
because it's still too close to home for comfort. Notoriety and public confes-
sion in literary form is a frazzler of the heart you were born with, believe me.

Interviewer: Allen said once that he learned how to read Shakespeare, that he
never did understand Shakespeare until he heard you read Shakespeare to him.
Kerouac: Because in a previous lifetime that's who I was.

> How like a Winter hath my absence been from thee?
> The pleasure of the fleeting year . . . what freezings
> have I felt? What dark days seen? Yet Summer with his
> lord surcease hath laid a big turd in my orchard
> And one hog after another comes to eat
> and break my broken mountain trap, and my mousetrap
> too! And here to end the sonnet, you must make sure
> to say, tara-tara-tara.....!!!!!!

Interviewer: Is that spontaneous composition?
Kerouac: Well, the first part was Shakespeare . . . and the second part was . . .

Interviewer: Have you ever written any sonnets?
Kerouac: I'll give you a spontaneous sonnet. It has to be what, now?

Interviewer: Fourteen lines.
Kerouac: That's twelve lines with two dragging lines. That's where you bring up your heavy artillery.

> Here the fish of Scotland seen your eye
> and all my nets did creak . . .

Does it have to rhyme?

Interviewer: No.
Kerouac:

> My poor chapped hands fall awry
> and seen the Pope, his devilled eye.
> And maniacs with wild hair hanging about my room
> and listening to my tomb
> which does not rhyme.
> Seven lines?

Interviewer: That was eight lines.
Kerouac:

> And all the orgones of the earth will crawl
> like dogs across the graves of Peru
> and Scotland too.

That's ten.

> Yet do not worry, sweet angel of mine
> That hast thine inheritance
> imbedded in mine.

Interviewer: That's pretty good, Jack. How did you do that?
Kerouac: Without studying dactyls . . . like Ginsberg . . . I met Ginsberg . . . I'd hitchhiked all the way back from Mexico City to Berkeley, and that's a long way baby, a long way. Mexico City across Durango . . . Chihuahua . . . Texas. I go back to Ginsberg, I go to his cottage, I say, "Hah, we're gonna play

the music" . . . he says, "You know what I'm going to do tomorrow? I'm going to throw on Mark Schorer's desk a new theory of prosody! About the dactyllic arrangements of Ovid!" (*Laughter*)

I said, "Quit, man. Sit under a tree and forget it and drink wine with me . . . and Phil Whalen and Gary Snyder and all the bums of San Francisco. Don't you try to be a big Berkeley teacher. Just be a poet under the trees . . . and we'll wrestle and we'll break holds." And he did take my advice. He remembered that. He said, "What are you going to teach . . . you have parched lips!" I said, "Naturally, I just came from Chihuahua. It's very hot down there, phew! you go out and little pigs rub against your legs. Phew!"

So here comes Snyder with a bottle of wine . . . and here comes Whalen, and here comes what's his name . . . Rexroth . . . and everybody . . . and we had the poetry renaissance of San Francisco.

Interviewer: What about Allen getting kicked out of Columbia? Didn't you have something to do with that?

Kerouac: Oh, no . . . he let me sleep in his room. He was not kicked out of Columbia for that. The first time he let me sleep in his room, and the guy that slept in our room with us was Lancaster who was descended from the White Roses or Red Roses of England. But a guy came in . . . the guy that ran the floor and he thought that I was trying to make Allen, and Allen had already written in the paper that I wasn't sleeping there because I was trying to make him, but he was trying to make me. But we were just actually sleeping. Then after that he got a pad . . . he got some stolen goods in there . . . and he got some thieves up there, Vicky and Huncke. And they were all busted for stolen goods, and a car turned over, and Allen's glasses broke, it's all in John Holmes's *Go*.

Allen Ginsberg asked me when he was nineteen years old, should I change my name to Allen Renard? You change your name to Allen Renard I'll kick you right in the balls! Stick to Ginsberg . . . and he did. That's one thing I like about Allen. Allen *Renard*!!!

Interviewer: What was it that brought all of you together in the '50s? What was it that seemed to unify the "Beat Generation"?

Kerouac: Oh the beat generation was just a phrase I used in the 1951 written manuscript of *On the Road* to describe guys like Moriarty who run around the country in cars looking for odd jobs, girlfriends, kicks. It was thereafter picked up by West Coast leftist groups and turned into a meaning like "beat mutiny" and "beat insurrection" and all that nonsense; they just wanted some youth movement to grab onto for their own political and social purposes. I had nothing to do with any of that. I was a football player, a scholarship college student, a merchant seaman, a railroad brakeman on road freights, a script synopsizer, a secretary . . . And Moriarty-Cassady was an actual cowboy on Dave Uhl's ranch in New Raymer Colorado . . . What kind of beatnik is that?

Interviewer: Was there any sense of "community" among the Beat crowd?
Kerouac: That community feeling was largely inspired by the same characters I mentioned, like Ferlinghetti, Ginsberg; they are very socialistically minded and want everybody to live in some kind of frenetic kibbutz, solidarity and all that. I was a loner. Snyder is not like Whalen, Whalen is not like McClure, I am not like McClure, McClure is not like Ferlinghetti, Ginsberg is not like Ferlinghetti, but we all had fun over wine anyway. We knew thousands of poets and painters and jazz musicians. There's no "beat crowd" like you say . . . what about Scott Fitzerald and his "lost crowd," does that sound right? Or Goethe and his "Wilhelm Meister crowd"? The subject is such a bore. Pass me that glass.

Interviewer: Well, why did they split in the early '60s?
Kerouac: Ginsberg got interested in left wing politics . . . like Joyce I say, as Joyce said to Ezra Pound in the 1920s, "Don't bother me with politics, the only thing that interests me is style." Besides I'm bored with the new avant-garde and the skyrocketing sensationalism. I'm reading Blaise Pascal and taking notes on religion. I like to hang around now with nonintellectuals, as you might call them, and not have my mind proselytized, ad infinitum. They've even started crucifying chickens in happenings, what's the next step? An actual crucifixion of a man . . . The beat group dispersed as you say in the early '60s, all went their own way, and this is my way: home life, as in the beginning, with a little toot once in a while in local bars.

Interviewer: What do you think of what they're up to now? Allen's radical political involvement? Burrough's cut-up methods?
Kerouac: I'm pro-American and the radical political involvements seem to tend elsewhere . . . The country gave my Canadian family a good break, more

or less, and we see no reason to demean said country. As for Burroughs's cut-up method, I wish he'd get back to those awfully funny stories of his he used to write and those marvelously dry vignettes in *Naked Lunch*. Cut-up is nothing new, in fact that steeltrap brain of mine does a lot of cutting up as it goes along . . . as does everyone's brain while talking or thinking or writing . . . It's just an old Dada trick, and a kind of literary collage. He comes out with some great effects though. I like him to be elegant and logical and that's why I don't like the cut-up which is supposed to teach us that the mind is cracked. Sure the mind's cracked, as anybody can see in a hallucinated high, but how about an explanation of the crackedness that can be understood in a workaday moment?

Interviewer: What do you think about the hippies and the LSD scene?
Kerouac: They're already changing. I shouldn't be able to make a judgment. And they're not all of the same mind. The Diggers are different . . . I don't know one hippie anyhow . . . I think they think I'm a truckdriver. And I am. As for LSD, it's bad for people with incidence of heart disease in the family. (*Knocks microphone off footstool . . . recovers it*)
      Is there any reason why you can see anything good in this yere mortality?

Interviewer: Excuse me, would you mind repeating that?
Kerouac: You said you had a little white beard in your belly. Why is there a little white beard in your mortality belly?

Interviewer: Let me think about it. Actually it's a little white pill.
Kerouac: A little white pill?

Interviewer: It's good.
Kerouac: Give me.

Interviewer: We should wait till the scene cools a little.
Kerouac: Right. This little white pill is a little white beard in your mortality which advises you and advertises to you that you will be growing long fingernails in the graves of Peru.
Saroyan: Do you feel middle-aged?
Kerouac: No. Listen, we're coming to the end of the tape. I want to add something on. Ask me what Kerouac means.

Interviewer: Jack, tell me again what Kerouac means.

Kerouac: Now, Kairn. K (or C) A-I-R-N. What is a kairn? It's a heap of stones. Now Cornwall, kairn-wall. Now, right, kern, also K-E-R-N, means the same thing as Kairn, Kern, Kairn. Ouac means language of. So, Kernuac means the language of Cornwall. Kerr, which is like Deborah Kerr . . . ouack means language of the water. Because Kerr, Carr, etc., means water. And Kairn means heap of stones. There is no language in a heap of stones. Kerouac. Ker-water, ouac-language of. And it's related to the old Irish name, Kerwick, which is a corruption. And it's a Cornish name, which in itself means Kairnish. And according to Sherlock Holmes, it's all Persian. Of course you know he's not Persian. Don't you remember in Sherlock Holmes when he went down with Dr. Watson and solved the case down in old Cornwall and he solved the case and then he said, "Watson, the needle! Watson, the needle . . ." He said, "I've solved this case here in Cornwall. Now I have the liberty to sit around here and decide and read books, which will prove to me . . . why the Cornish people, otherwise known as the Kernuaks, or Kerouacs, are of Persian origin. The enterprise which I am about to embark upon," he then said, after he got his shot, "is fraught with eminent peril, and not fit for a lady of your tender years." Remember that?

Mc Naughton: I remember that.

Kerouac: McNaughton remembers that. McNaughton. You think I would forget the name of a Scotsman?

Off the Road: The Celtic Twilight of Jack Kerouac

Gregory McDonald / 1968

The house in Hyannis has already been let and there's a FOR SALE sign plastered on the $30,000 development house in Lowell. In what was designed to be the dining room of that house lies his mother, the skin of her face as smooth as a baby's, her left side paralyzed by a stroke two years ago. All she wants is to move to St. Petersburg, Florida, where a house is waiting for them. "I know Jackie's trying very hard to get some money, but I don't know." A few feet away in the living room, just the other side of a thin plastic folding-accordian door, facing the other way, sits Jack Kerouac in a rocking chair, red slippers, white socks, pajama pants, open plaid flannel shirt, T-shirt over a big belly, still bigger chest, not having shaved or eaten for four days, not since we had arranged to do this thing, "Completely surrounded by booze," in his own words, averaging twelve to fifteen shots of whiskey and gulps of beer an hour, seven feet from his own television set, staring at the midday pap, his mind as sensitive as a frog's opened heart, talking.

"If I didn't have my Scotch and beer I wouldn't speak to anybody."

Over the mantelpiece, to the right of his television, is a fine pencil drawing of his brother, who died at the age of nine of rheumatic fever, done by a German, which drawing is on the cover of a Kerouac book, *Visions of Gerard,* "which nobody reads any more. It's too sad." On the wall behind Kerouac is a painting called *Night Wash,* done by a friend, which is exactly that, a literal pun. Directly over his head is a painting of Pope Paul as a cardinal (copied from *Life* magazine eight years ago) by Kerouac himself.

"Painting's my hobby. I don't like to do it. It makes my hands dirty."

In the background, the present Mrs. Kerouac, Stella (Jack's first marriage was annulled, his second ended in divorce; he was married for the third time in Hyannis, November 1966), moves from the dining room to the kitchen to the living room, nursing them both, getting coffee for me, helping things to be understood, arranging for the lawn to be fertilized, giving Greek cookies to a young man who comes to the door, for his mother, collecting what pictures they have for us to use with this story.

"I absolutely will not be photographed," Kerouac said. "I couldn't stand it."

"It's all right, Jackie. There will be no photographers. He promised."

"I guess I wouldn't have made a soldier. My theory is to give all the soldiers belts with bottles of whiskey hanging from them. That way they'd win the battle. Makes you sentimental. Everybody would look out for his buddy."

Two months before, his brother-in-law, who had been a World War II army sergeant, went on a sentimental trip back to Europe. He took Kerouac with him, thinking that way he would get red-carpet treatment everywhere he went. They were thrown out of several places. Among other things, Jack paid a prostitute in Portugal named Linda ten dollars to stare into his eyes for a solid hour by the clock. Then he gave her another ten.

In Germany, Kerouac became fascinated by the way the Aryan types walked along the street.

He got up to strut, march, goose-step up and down the living room sixteen times in hilarious imitation. The narrow, modern living room was full of the movement of this 198 pound bear of a man.

"I came back to America saying the poor Jews."

We had arranged that I would stick with him as long as I could and write everything down and print it because he is sick of people interviewing him and then printing nothing. He no longer grants interviews. In fact, writing now, I know I cannot print everything he said, because of space and because sometimes you cannot do what you promise.

Staring at the continuous daytime pap, taking constant Scotch and beer: "I want to be commissioned to do my next book, which will be called *Beat Spotlight*. I want $5000 advance on that and $5000 advance on *Visions of Cody* so I can get the hell out of here and get to Florida. The people here are nice. The water's no good."

His last book, published only a few months ago by Coward-McCann, *Vanity of Duluoz* (three syllables; Du-lu-oz: the louse; Kerouac: the cockroach), is autobiography, from his Lowell boyhood to prep school in New York, Columbia University, the Navy, the Merchant Marine, to the point where he went on the road. It's a good book.

About 10 percent of *Cody* was published in a limited edition in 1960.

"The *Compleat Visions of Cody*. Not published yet. I wrote it sixteen years ago, in 1952. Ginsberg told me it's the masterpiece of all ages. It's a fantastic poem. A 512-page paean to a cowboy I once knew, Cody, whose real name is Neal Cassady, who was the Moriarity in *On the Road*. I've changed his name now four or five times.

"You know, a little magazine on the West Coast is saying that he died trying to live up to the image I created for him. A crock of. The fact is, he's not even dead. It's a trick."

"Jack, you don't know he's not dead," Stella said. "His wife said so."

"I think he's in Spain. Mexico's a big place, too. It's just a trick to get out from his wife."

"You'll see him, Jack."

"I don't mean transcendental things. I think he might be dead. Last time I saw him he was ranting. Do you want to hear how he talked?"

Jack then did an imitation of how Cassady had talked four years ago: irrationally.

"I said, 'Why haven't you changed, Cassady? You're still stupid!' He was losing control. They got him a bus, flowers painted all over it that said NOWHERE on it. And he drove the bus from California to New Orleans to New York. Fifty couples playing guitars and throwing flowers out the windows. They had a microphone in front of his face and he talked all the way onto tape from California to New York. No wonder he went mad.

"We met Ginsberg in the East Village and he said, 'Let's go to a party,' and I said, 'Who's going to be there?' and Ginsberg said, 'Ken Kesey, there are movies and lights and dancing on the flag.' Ginsberg put the flag around my shoulders and I took it off and folded it up and put it over the sofa. I was disgusted and I still am.

"America was an idea that was proposed and began to deteriorate at the turn of the century when people came in waving flags. And now their grandchildren dance on the flag. Damn them."

Reading Kerouac's great books of the Beat generation, *On the Road*, *The Dharma Bums*, *Big Sur*, you wonder what has happened to the beatnik characters as you wonder what happens to the leaders of any exuberant, youth-freedom movement beatnik, hippy-yip, once youth is gone, fifteen years later.

"Neal Cassady's wife, Carolyn, called Jack February 4, a few months ago, and told him they had found Neal dead beside a railroad track in Mexico," Stella said to me. "Coincidentally enough, February 4 is his mother's, Memere's birthday."

According to Kerouac's own account, he has written eighteen books, which have been translated into eighteen languages and published in forty-three countries. His income this year (he is forty-six) averages $60 a week.

The most he ever made from a book was $40,000, off *On the Road*, which was heavily taxed. (A writer's income, like a boxer's, unlike the income of a man who simply digs the recourses of the earth, like oil, is taxed as straight income in this country in the year he receives it, regardless of how many years it took him to make it, or how impossible it would be for him to make it again. Publicized improvements in the tax laws have had little practical effect upon the incomes of many writers.) Much of the rest was used paying for his mother's interminable north-south-north moves. Only *The Subterraneans* was bought for a movie, from which he profited little.

"Why should they buy *On the Road* when they can steal it?" Stella asked. "Did you ever see that television program?"

Jack said, "In New York it is quite common to make light of someone who is honest and not demanding."

In that morning's mail had been a letter from his agent saying Kerouac owed him $157. There had also been a letter from some creeps in Oregon saying they were going to have a seance to contact the spirit of Neal Cassady, and it might be easier if Kerouac were there. When his wife read this letter to him, Kerouac shrieked, "On my magic carpet I will fly!"

He jumped up. "I want you to note that besides being a great painter and a great writer, I'm a great pianist and composer."

He then sat down at the upright.

"You'll only wake up Memere, Jack."

And played notes and chords. "God Rest Ye Merry Gentlemen is a Cornish folk tune," he said. "I'm Cornish."

"He saw a Cornish movie on television last night," Stella said. "With Rex Harrison."

He sat in his rocker again and I asked why he had never spent much time in Europe. He put his head in his hands. He said, slowly, "I'd like to have a little farm in Southern France, like Picasso."

I should have told you before this that every time Kerouac speaks, with painful self-consciousness he uses a different accent, high British, Cockney, Southern, Irish, Southwestern.

"Why don't you tell him the truth, Jack, why you've never lived in Europe?"

He got up heavily. "Because I'm an American pioneer."

She said, "He can't get enough of it, that's all."

He came back down the stairs with two slim boxes in his hand.

"You want to know why I like America. I'll tell you why."

Sitting in his rocker, hunched over, eyes closed, he played *Across the Wide Missouri* on one of the two harmonicas so sweetly in the midday shade of the room it would have made Uncle Ho love America. He played a sort of flamenco on the other harmonica: "That covers Mexico." And *O, Canada* on the first harmonica, sort of wetly. "And that covers Canada."

"He just can't get enough of it," she said. "This country."

"The American Civil Liberties Union is Communist. The police are afraid to arrest genuine malefactors." He opened the window behind my head and gently waved a bug out of it. "My brother taught me that," he said, indicating the drawing of the nine-year-old boy over the fireplace. "All they arrest is harmless drunks like me.

"I came to Lowell because I thought I was coming home again. America used to be a pretty good country. Kids used to hang themselves at Camp Lee in 1942–43, rather than be sent overseas."

Much of Kerouac's short time in the service was spent in a Naval mental hospital. Any real action he saw was in the Merchant Marine.

From his rocker, he pointed to my car through the window, "Is that your car? I can drive, but I've never had a license. I can drive on the highway, but not downtown. All my friends are the best drivers. Neal driving me 3000 miles across this country, all the time looking me in the eyes.

"I'm afraid of cars. I'm not afraid of horses. Horses can fight back. Cars might hit somebody."

He then did an imitation, complete with mouth noises of horses' hoof beats, of a lancer on a horse.

"I'm afraid of all machines. I have machineophobia. My mother can only sleep in the back seat when I'm at the wheel."

The family car is a thirteen-year-old black Ford coupe.

"How do you write?" I asked. "Is it much trouble for you to get yourself up for it?"

"As Saint Mathew says, Do not store up in your mind what you will say, for it is the Holy Ghost Who speaks through you. I don't write. The Holy Ghost writes through me. You're surprised, aren't you? This is the first time you've ever met the Holy Ghost in person. I do a certain mechanical thing. But I am the Holy Ghost speaking."

"What purpose are you serving through the Holy Ghost?"

"I'm taking orders from heaven. In heaven sits God. On His left, Mary. On His right, Jesus. In front of Them, the golden baby of paradise: Jackie Kerouac. I have a high opinion of myself, right? I'm serious. I was sent here to do something."

"What are you doing?"

"I'm a messenger. I didn't want to come here. May I remind you that you have never seen my Father's face? I have seen His face. I am the brother of Jesus. We're a very holy Family. Incidentally, my mother is a descendant of Napoleon."

"You're a messenger. What's the message?"

"The message from heaven? That after we die we're all raised to the highest part of heaven, no matter what we do, as a fitting reward to answer Lucifer's plea to fall from heaven. Lucifer comes to us in heaven, you see, and says, 'You like it up here, Jackie? Couldn't things be better?' You say, 'Yeah, maybe,' and Tha-wong! you're born. But it couldn't be better. Beds of roses. Clouds making refreshing faces all day long.

"Religion, senor, is your own broken heart.

"You think I'm insane, don't you? I am insane. All American authors are insane. You have to be crazy to be a writer in this country."

While Kerouac tried to get his agent on the phone (he was "out of the country" that day) I talked with Jack's mother about Florida and looked at some paintings Stella brought up from the basement, one by Gregory Corso, six or seven by Jack, one of which was bright and happy. Stella said he had done it while on mescaline. Jack then talked with his publisher. Give me $5000 on *Compleat Visions of Cody* and $5000 on *Beat Spotlight* so I can get my mother to Florida and get to work on *Beat Spotlight*. Listen. Give me no money. Just publish *Compleat Visions of Cody*. Ginsberg says it's an important book." Jack then allowed me to understand the publishers are not too keen on *The Compleat Visions of Cody*. "It's always been too dirty," he said.

Stella tried to induce him to stay home by reminding him that the Merv Griffin Show started at four-thirty. While I had been upstairs for a minute, Jack had sort of dressed in trousers, shoes, a windbreaker and a pork-pie hat.

On the sidewalk he screamed at kids playing basketball in the next driveway to shut up and when they looked terrified at him he gave them the raspberry.

In the car, I said, "How come you've never been able to finish anything, a year of school, a football season, yet you have been able to finish so many books?"

"I don't finish. I just write it continuously. Sooner or later you reach the point in a book where you feel everybody's bored, and you bring it around somehow and end it. That's deep form."

He entered every bar shouting ferociously, "I'm Kerouac!" In every bar in Lowell, following his nose sideways across every street, Kerouac is known.

"When you first thought of writing when you were a kid, what kind of a writer did you think you were going to be?"

"I thought I was going to be Mark Twain."

"In your own mind, what kind of a writer are you?"

"A naturalistic. Like Dreiser. A German Romanticist. Write 'em both down. A Celtic twilight."

"Anybody writing today better than you are?"

"No. Not since Shakespeare. When he went out for a beer in the afternoon people called him Sweet Will. They should call me Sweet Jack. Except maybe Laurence Sterne." Beside his chair at the house was a book by Laurence Sterne. "Maybe George Herbert."

He had taken five dollars from his wife before he left the house. Second bar we were in he gave a kid named Morris one dollar for shining his shoes.

"What do you think of Norman Mailer?"

"He's an ugly and ridiculous man."

To everybody's amusement and disdain, watering the corner of nearly every redbrick building he passed, Kerouac pursued sleep through every bar in Lowell. At some point in our progress a kindly cop named Pasquale, "Pat," cigar held in a toothless gap in the front of his mouth, told me about the time Jack had seen three pedigree dogs through a pet shop window, a malamute, a collie and something else, and had bought all three at once to have them drag him through the bars.

"What were you so vain about, Duluoz?"

"Beating everybody athletically and by scholarship."

He recited Emily Dickinson in the green bars, most of which looked like stage sets for a play by William Alfred, shamrocks everywhere, tall and short men called Councilor, Commissioner in shiny suits standing up at the bar, talking about ward politics, who is in, who is out, and, of jail, scowling at the half-staffed trousers of this man they grew up with who carries a bit of the world (he knows where Oregon is and Oregon knows where he is) and a lot of books on the weight of his breath.

"What would have happened to you, Jack, if you had never left Lowell?"

"I would have worked in a mill all my life."

He shouted nonsense tone poems of his own, (Beejeebeejee) the personal meanings of which brought tears to his own eyes, wide-set, gray-blue, as different from each other as the tragi-comic masks, and pleadingly expressive. He took literary advice from everybody we met, every cop, fly and broad, that he should write, and when, and about what, saying only, each time, his wide and handsome grin beneath four day's gray stubble: "You know what? It's weird but what he says is true."

What he wanted to fight about was whether or not Al Mello was the best boxer ever to come out of Lowell. The first time he punched me he had the preppie's grace to grab his workman's square, intellectual's soft hand and say "Ouch!" as if he meant it, and the second time he hit me more softly. I think he wanted to say that he had been the best boxer, the best anything, to have come out of Lowell. Then he sprayed me with wet laughter.

"Have you ever felt one-to-one with anyone, Jack?"

"Yes, Neal Cassady. He can't be dead. Oh, God. He can't be dead."

At the house he had said, "I don't speak with an accent all the time. I've got to get out of here."

"Have you ever been yourself with anyone, Jack?"

"I know another bar."

I was to leave him, asleep, sitting at a bar owned by his brother-in-law.

"Religion, senor, is your own broken heart."

"What about it?"

"That's a beautiful line, Sweet Jack."

Some day, I pray to Kerouac's God, this country that Kerouac loves so much will grow up just enough to realize that what writers do is Man's hardest, most exhausting, self-destructive work, as their only tool in etching the hard lines of history on stone is themselves and must be used until blunted, and will pay them a decent wage for what they do, grant them at least the comfort and security, the dignity of Pasternak's country *dacha*, and not require them to be performing apes, speaking in accents, playing instruments, proposing weird philosophies and doing comic imitations, to attain for themselves the dead man's grace.

Jack Kerouac Is on the Road No More

Jack McClintock / 1969

From *St. Petersburg Times*, October 12, 1969, *Floridian* sec., pp. 4, 6–10.
Copyright *St. Petersburg Times* 1969. Reprinted with permission.

"But then they danced down the street like dinglebodies, and I shambled after
as I've been doing all my life after people who interest me, because the only people
for me are the mad ones, the ones who are mad for life, mad to talk, mad to
be saved, desirous of everything at the same time, the ones who never yawn or
say a commonplace thing but burn, burn, burn like fabulous yellow roman
candles exploding like spiders across the stars and in the middle you see the
blue centerlight pop and everybody goes 'Awww!' "

—From *On the Road* by Jack Kerouac

What happens to a Beatnik in the age of Aquarius?

Some, like Allen Ginsberg, accommodate to the times and become gurus,
Om-ing their way from campus to campus, demonstration to demonstration.

But what of those other cult heroes of the fifties, those picturesque, pica-
resque, poetic wanderers of the open road, the Beats? The Corsos, the
Cassadys, the Ferlinghettis?

And what of Jack Kerouac, the king of them all, the king of *On the Road*?

He is forty-six. He lives in St. Petersburg with his third wife Stella and his
paralyzed mother. The house, neat concrete and brick, is his mother's.

"I don't go out much anymore," he says. "I don't really go out at all." Nor
does he particularly seek publicity.

When a photographer was assigned to get a picture of Kerouac recently,
Stella answered the door and said, "He's sick. He'll call you when he feels better."

He never called.

A week or so later a reporter walked between the palms by the sidewalk
and knocked on the same door. Stella, a gray-haired woman with a wide, sad
smile, said: "He's not home."

And then a face came peering over Stella's shoulder. A face with grizzled jowls and red-rimmed eyes under spikey, dark tousled hair. Kerouac? The face said, "Yeah," and then: "You want to come in?"

Although the sun was two hours from taking its evening dip in the Gulf ten miles to the west, the house was dim inside. A television set in the corner was on, soundless. The sound you heard was Handel's *Messiah* blaring from speakers in the next room.

"I like to watch television like that," Kerouac said.

"You ain't going to take my photo, are you? You better not try to take my photo or I'll kick your ass." A threatening leer, then a laugh.

"Stella, *Hey!* Turn the music up!" Stella went and turned the music up. Her feet were silent on the floor.

Kerouac dragged up a rocking chair for the reporter, then slumped into another one in the corner.

He was wearing unpressed brown pants, a yellow-and-brown striped sport shirt, with the sleeves rolled to the elbow. The shirt was unbuttoned and beneath it the T-shirt was inside out. He pointed to his belly, large and round.

"I got a goddam hernia, you know that? My goddam bellybutton is popping out. That's why I'm dressed like this . . . I got no place to go, anyway. You want a beer? Hah?" He picked up a pack of Camels in a green plastic case. "Some whiskey then?"

What was he doing these days, Kerouac was asked.

"Well, I wrote that article," he said, a trifle belligerently. His agent was busy selling a piece Kerouac had written, entitled "After Me, the Deluge," his reflections on today's world and what he might have contributed to it.

Anything else?

"Well, I'm going to write a novel about the last ten years of my life . . ."

He's been living here a couple years this time; before that a while in Lowell, Massachusetts, his hometown, and Hyannis. It's hard to get a conventional history from Kerouac, who is bored by such commonplace matters.

"I get lonely here. I live with my mother; she's in the back room, paralyzed. Are you writing all this down? God bless the Celts, write that down. Tell them to pronounce it like it was a K."

He pursed his lips way out, and rolled his eyes.

"I can beat you up, that's why I talk so tough." Then he gave an astonishingly sheepish, little-boy grin, and said: "I hope."

He leaned back and reached for his beer can.

And here is Jack Kerouac, the man who in his lifetime has been the idol of thousands of kids who grew up envying his football prowess at Columbia University, his tossing all that aside to go on the road, his earnest, tumbling, manic "spontaneous" prose when he wrote about it all in *On the Road*, *The Dharma Bums*, *The Subterraneans* and other autobiographical novels. There were seventeen books, he says, translated into forty-seven languages.

A Kerouac cult grew up. The cultists read all that he wrote, all that all the Beats wrote. They knew the esoterica. Moriarity was really Cassady. Cody was really Cassady. Hart Kennedy was Cassady. Neal Cassady seemed the inspiration of the Beat Generation, though he wrote little himself.

The Beat Generation. The fifties.

"John Clellan Holmes says one day, 'So we had the Lost Generation and the...'

"And I said, 'We're the Beat Generation,'" Kerouac says. "That was in 1948."

The Cult of the Beats was only one such, perhaps the first. Later, kids erected the same sort of mythology around Salinger's *The Catcher in the Rye* (with a splinter cult digging instead William Goldman's *Temple of Gold*), then around Golding's *Lord of the Flies*, and then Ken Kesey's *One Flew over the Cuckoo's Nest*. And Kesey had his troops, too, the Merry Pranksters, a latter-day collection of followers and hangers-on just like Kerouac's pals.

They included Neal Cassady, and that brought it full circle.

"I don't like Ken Kesey," Kerouac says today. "He ruined Cassady."

Cassady is said to be dead now. "He's supposed to be dead, but I don't believe it."

And here is Kerouac sitting in a rocking chair in a corner of this dim living room and watching Cronkite moving his lips on the silent screen. He hasn't shaved in a day or two and there is gray in the whiskers. "I'm really Wallace Beery in *The Champ*," he grins.

There is a half-quart can of Falstaff at his elbow, and he is sipping whiskey from one of those medicine vials with the white plastic top you snap off, snap back on.

Snap. Sip. Snap, it goes, very regularly, a neat and tidy sound. Snap.

"Call me Mr. Boilermaker. I get lonesome here... You know how much I made this year? Between January 1 and July 1, $1,770. That's what I made. But I just got $3,000 last week."

He was on the Buckley show a while back with two other guests, a student and a sociologist, "Yeah, two Communists." (Later, during another conversation, he said, "The Mafia? The Communist is the main enemy—the Jew.")

On the program they talked about the Beat Generation a little, but mostly about the hippies and the political activists of today. Kerouac doesn't care much for today.

"Yeah, they got something from us–they just took it too far. The Communist Party jumped on my movement, they wanted a youth movement to use."

"Ginsberg . . . At a party with Kesey's Merry Pranksters Ginsberg came up and wrapped an American flag around me. So I took it (Kerouac demonstrates how he took it, and the movements are tender) and I folded it up the way you're supposed to, and put it on the back of the sofa. The flag is not a rag.

"When we went to school together, we were twenty-one and it was books and Shakespeare. But now Ginsberg's anti-American."

Was the beat thing an alcohol trip, the way the hippie thing is a drug trip?

"I smoked more grass than anyone you ever knew in your life," Kerouac snorts. "I came across the Mexican border one time with 2½ pounds of grass around my waist in a silk scarf. I had one of those wide Mexican belts around me over it. I had a big bottle of tequila and I went up to the border guard and offered him some, and he said, No, go on through, senor."

Kerouac laughed, remembering how that was.

"It should be legalized and taxed. Taxed. Yeah, 'Gimme a pack of marijuana!' But this other stuff is poison; acid's poison, speed is poison, STP is poison, it's all poison. But grass is nothing."

He gets up and goes to the kitchen for another beer, and on the way back he stops to replay the record. The record comes on playing at 78 rpm. Kerouac walks across the room, slumps into the rocker, neatly picks up the conversation where he had left it.

The *Messiah* sounds high, fast and silly, like those Alvin the Chipmunk songs a few years ago.

Stella glides through the room and sighs. "Oh Jackie," and fixes the record.

Kerouac points to an oil painting on the wall. "You know who that is?"

It was Pope Paul, with big blue eyes.

"You like that, don't you? Guess who painted it. Me."

He had said earlier, "I'm not a beatnik. I'm a Catholic."

"I just sneak into church now, at dusk, at vespers. But yeah, as you get older you get more . . . genealogical."

Kerouac wanted to talk about the article he had written, which was selling rather well to Sunday magazines in major cities in the U.S.

"It's about the Communist conspiracy," he said. He eyed the reporter narrowly, and when satisfied with the lack of response, began to read. The article was typed on yellow legal paper. He read with broad, wild gestures, grinning and mugging and assuming various foreign accents. The voice went up high, dropped confidentially low. It sped along, it dragged portentously. And the words had an unusual eloquence, the allusions were astonishingly erudite, the sounds made a lush and rich cadence, all coming from this man with bare feet and two days' growth of salt-and-pepper whiskers.

It was a wondrous performance, so much so that the reporter came away without the vaguest notion of what the article might have been about.

"I'm glad to see you 'cause I'm very lonesome here," he said, and then talked for a moment about the proposed new novel.

"Stories of the past," said Jack Kerouac. "My story is endless. I put in a tele-type roll, you know, you know what they are, you have them in newspapers, and run it through there and fix the margins and just go, go—just go, go, go."

Cody (Neal Cassady) you are, I believe, my last remaining pal—I don't think I'll ever have another like you for I might retire in (like Swenson) so far, or go crazy or eccentric—of course somewhere along the line I'll end up yakking with some wench in a black night, like Louis Ferdinand Celine, like those lonely soldiers who came back from Germany with six-foot-ten-years-older-than-them Isolde warbrides and argue with them in bleak rooms over drugstores, in bars, on church steps, in the middle of the night in winter...

—From *Visions of Cody*

Index

"Across the Wide Missouri," 86
Albee, Edward, xviii
Alfred, William, 89
Allen, Don, 23
Alvin and the Chipmunks, 94
And the Hippos Were Boiled in Their Tanks
    (Burroughs and Kerouac), 60
Ansen, Alan, 60
Apollinaire, Guillaume, 64
Aristophanes, 46
Aronowitz, Al, xiii–xiv, 10–36; *Blacklisted*
    Masterpieces, 10
Auden, W. H., 62

Bach, Johann Sebastian, 4, 61
Balzac, Honoré de, xi, 44; *Comédie Humaine*,
    xviii
Baudelaire, Charles, 24
Beery, Wallace, 93
Beethoven, Ludwig van, 28
Berrigan, Ted, 51–81
Billboard, 21
Blacklisted Masterpieces (Aronowitz), 10
Blake, Caroline Kerouac, xx, 16, 20, 36, 43
Bomb, The (Corso), 39
Boston Sunday Globe, 82
Brierly, Justin W., 35
Buckley, William F., Jr, 94
Buddha, 13, 26, 38, 47, 67 68 70, 74
Burns, George, 64
Burroughs, William S., xix, xx, 8, 28–29, 33, 60,
    63, 66, 75, 79–80; *And the Hippos Were*
    Boiled in Their Tanks, 60; *Junkie*, 61; *Naked*
    Lunch, xx, 60, 80
Butler, Nicholas Murray, 28

Campanella, Roy, 41
Cannastra, Bill, 30, 33–34, 61–62
Capote, Truman, 13, 16, 33, 49

Carson, Johnny, 67
Cassady, Carolyn, 85
Cassady, Neal, xii, xiii, xv, xix, xxi, 8, 16, 24, 34–35,
    36, 38, 54–56, 62–63, 79, 84–85, 89, 91, 93;
    The First Third, 54; *Joan Anderson Letter*, 54
Catcher in the Rye (Salinger), 93
Cayce, Edgar, 62
Celine, Louis Ferdinand, 24, 95
Cervantes Saavedra, Miguel de, 32
Champ, The (Vidor), 93
Chaplin, Charlie, xvi, 35
Chase, Hal, 35
Chevalier, Maurice, 22
Chicago Daily News, 43
Citizen Kane (Welles), xiii–xiv, 26
Clemens, Samuel L., 54, 88
Comédie Humaine (Balzac), xviii
Corso, Gregory, 8–9, 32, 34, 39, 63, 64, 87, 91;
    The Bomb, 39; *Gasoline*, 8
Cotten, Joseph, xiv, 26
Cowley, Malcolm, 20, 31, 35, 53, 54, 66
Crowley, Aleister, 53

Daring Young Man on the Flying Trapeze, The
    (Saroyan), 65
Devadatta, 69
Dickinson, Emily, xvii, 32, 34, 89
Dolce Vita, La (Fellini), 56
Dostoyevsky, Fyodor, 13, 34, 35, 36, 54; *The Life*
    of a Great Sinner, 54; *Notes from the*
    Underground, 55
Doyle, Arthur Conan, 81
Dreiser, Theodore, 54, 88
Duncan, Val, xi, xiii, 37–39, 46–50

Eddy, George, 12, 23
Eddy, Mona Kent, 12, 19, 23; *Portia Faces Life*, 12
Eddy, Nelson, 23
Emerson, Ralph Waldo, 34

Esquire, xvi
Evergreen Review, 15

Fadiman, Clifton, 17
Fellini, Federico, *La Dolce Vita*, 56
Ferlinghetti, Lawrence, xx, 9, 79, 91
Fifth Symphony (Shostakovich), 47
Finnegans Wake (Joyce), 48
First Third, The (Cassady), 54
Fitzgerald, F. Scott, 7, 79
Frank, Robert, *Pull My Daisy*, 36

Gabin, Jean, 22
Gallimard, G. Claude, 22
Garver, Bill, 33
Gasoline (Corso), 8
Gaugin, Paul, 46
Genet, Jean, *Our Lady of the Flowers*, 63
Ginsberg, Allen, xii, xv, xix, 8, 11, 23–24, 26,
    28–29, 30, 31, 32–33, 34, 35, 38, 39, 46, 54,
    58, 60, 63, 66, 75–76, 77–78, 79, 84, 87, 91,
    94; *Howl*, 11, 32, 39
"God Rest Ye Merry Gentlemen," 85
Goethe, Johann Wolfgang von, 54; *Wilhelm
    Meister*, 79
Golding, William, *Lord of the Flies*, 93
Goldman, William, *The Temple of Gold*, 93
Gotama, 67
Graham, John, *System and Dialectics of Art*, xvii
Grant, Cary, xiii
Griffin, Merv, 88

Händel, George Frideric, 70; *Messiah*, 92, 94
Harrison, Rex, 85
Haverty, Joan, xix, 30
Hemingway, Ernest, 7, 20, 61, 66
Herbert, George, 88
Highlight, 7
Ho Chi Minh, 86
Holiday, 23
Holmes, John Clellon, 7, 16, 30, 73, 93; *Go*,
    61, 78
Homer, 35
Hui Neng, 67
Huncke, Herbert, xix, 28, 31, 78

Isaacs, Stan, xviii, 10, 40–42

Jamison, Joyce, 21
Jesus, 5, 68, 87
Joan Anderson Letter (Cassady), 54
Johnny Carson Show, 67
Joyce, James, 79; *Finnegans Wake*, 48; *Ulysses*, 48
Jubilee, 43
Junkie (Burroughs), 61

Kafka, Franz, 12
Kallman, Chester, 62
Kasyapa, 67
Kennedy, John F., 52
Kerouac, Caroline (sister), xx, 16, 20, 36, 43
Kerouac, Edie Parker (first wife), xix, 28, 29
Kerouac, Gabrielle (mother), xix, xxi, 11, 16–26,
    29, 36, 45, 47–48, 85, 86, 91
Kerouac, Gerard (brother), xix, 16
Kerouac, Jack
    Works and Projected Works: "After Me, the
        Deluge," 92; "An American Passed Here," 49;
        And the Hippos Were Boiled in Their Tanks,
        60; "Beat Generations," 36; "Beat Spotlight,"
        83, 87; *Big Sur*, xxi, 43, 44, 49, 50, 55, 84;
        Book of Dreams, xiii, xxi, 19, 55; *Desolation
        Angels*, xi, xx, xxi, 36, 44; *The Dharma
        Bums*, xi, xvi, xx, 7, 20, 21, 25, 33, 34, 37,
        38–39, 43, 44, 49, 53, 84, 93; *Dr. Sax*, xi,
        xiii, xxi, 12, 22, 34, 52, 66–67; "Legend of
        Duluoz," xvii–xviii, 44, 50; *Lonesome
        Traveler*, xi, xviii, xxi, 43; *Maggie Cassidy*,
        xx, xxi, 43; "Memory Babe," 49; *Mexico City
        Blues*, xx, xxi, 73; "October in Railroad
        Earth," 10, 15, 53, 55; *On the Road*, x, xi, xii,
        xv, xvi, xix, xx, 3, 7, 15, 16, 18, 20, 21, 25, 30,
        31, 32, 33–34, 35, 36, 37, 38, 43, 48–49, 52,
        53, 54, 55, 70, 71, 76, 78, 84, 85, 91, 93;
        Passing Through, 44; *Pull My Daisy*, 36;
        Rimbaud, 52; *Satori in Paris*, xvi, xxi, 55;
        The Subterraneans, xi, xiii, xx, 7, 20, 21, 24,
        26, 43, 55, 70, 71, 76, 85, 93; "Thrashing
        Doves," 52; *The Town and the City*, xii, xv,
        xix, 17–18, 24, 27, 29, 30, 34, 43, 52, 60;
        Tristessa, xx, xxi, 43, 52, 55, 71–72; *Vanity
        of Duluoz*, xxi, 44, 51, 55, 75, 76, 83–84;
        Visions of Cody, xi, xv, xxi, 52, 55, 62, 83, 84,
        87–88, 95; *Visions of Gerard*, xi, xviii, xx, xxi,
        16, 43–45, 49, 82; *Visions of Neal*, 16, 33, 36
Kerouac, Jan (daughter), xx

Kerouac, Jean-Baptiste (grandfather), 49
Kerouac, Joan Haverty (second wife), xix, 30
Kerouac, Leo (father), xix, 18, 25
Kerouac, Stella Sampas (third wife), xxi, 51–52, 83–88, 91–92
Kerr, Deborah, 81
Kesey, Ken, xxi, 84, 94; *One Flew over the Cuckoo's Nest*, 93; *Sometimes a Great Notion*, x
Kilgallen, Dorothy, 11
Kline, Franz, xvi
Kobayashi, Issa, 67

Lamantia, Philip, 6
Li Po, 26
Life, 15, 82
Life of a Great Sinner, The (Dostoyevsky), 54
Little, Lou, 14, 27, 59
Loewinsohn, Ronny, 9
Lord, Sterling, 11
Lord of the Flies (Golding), 93
Louis XIV, 22
Lowell, Robert, 63

MacDonald, Gregory, xvii, 82–90
MacDougall, Ranald, *The Subterraneans*, 21, 85
Mademoiselle, 26
Mailer, Norman, xvi, 29, 88
Marx, Groucho, 39
Marx, Harpo, 12
Marx, Karl, 39
Matsuo, Basho, 67
Matthew, Saint, 87
Mazur, Henry, 27
McClintock, Jack, xvii, 91–95
McClure, Mike, 8, 79
McLuhan, Marshall, 56
McNaughton, Duncan, 51, 81
Melanctha (Stein), 63
Mello, Al, 89
Melville, Herman, xvi, 10, 54
Mercurian, Everard, 68
Merv Griffin Show, The, 88
Messiah (Händel), 92, 94
Miller, Henry, xiii, 24; *Tropic of Cancer*, 24
Mohrt, Michel, 22, 23
Müller, Dody, 30
My Name Is Aram (Saroyan), 66

Naked Lunch (Burroughs), xx, 60
New York Post, xiii, 3–6, 15, 63
New York Times, 7, 12, 14, 30
Newsday, xi, xviii, 10, 37, 40, 46
Nightbeat (Wingate), xii
Notes from the Underground (Dostoyevsky), 55

"O, Canada," 86
Olson, Charles, 66, 72
One Flew over the Cuckoo's Nest (Kesey), 93
Orlovsky, Peter, 34, 63; "Second Poem," 63
Our Lady of the Flowers (Genet), 63
Ovid, 78

Padget, Ron, 52
Paris Review, xi–xii, xiv–xv, 51
Parker, Edie, xix, 28, 29
Pascal, Blaise, 79
Pasternak, Boris Leonidovich, 90
Persky, Stan, 9
Picasso, Pablo, 46, 86
Poe, Edgar Allan, 26
Pollock, Jackson, xvii
Pope Paul, 82, 94
Portia Faces Life (Eddy), 12
Pound, Ezra, 79
Proust, Marcel, xi, 44
Pull My Daisy (Frank), 36

Rabelais, François, 24
Rexroth, Kenneth, xiii, xx, 8, 9, 78
Rimbaud, Arthur, 34
Rosset, Barney, 22
Rouault, Georges, 46
Rousseau, Henri, 46
Ruth, Babe, 40

Sahl, Mort, 21
Salinger, J. D., *Catcher in the Rye*, 93
Sampas, Nick, xxi, 83
Sampas, Sebastian, 29
Sampas, Stella, xxi, 51–52, 83–88, 91–92, 94
Sampas, Tony, xxi, 83
San Francisco Beat, 7, 13
San Francisco Examiner, 7–9
Saroyan, Aram, 51, 52, 64–65, 68, 70, 71, 74–75
Saroyan, William, 65–66, 75; *The Daring Young Man on the Flying Trapeze*, 65; *My Name Is*

Aram, 66; *The Summer of the Beautiful White Horse*, 65–66
Sartre, Jean-Paul, 63
Schopenhauer, Arthur, 35
Schorer, Mark, 78
Schwaner, Jim, xv–xvi
Shakespeare, William, xvi, 34, 35, 48, 76, 88, 94
Sheresky, Dick, 15
Shiki, 56, 67
Shostakovich, Dmitri Dmitrievich, *Fifth Symphony*, 47
Sinatra, Frank, 11
Sixty Minutes, xiii
Snyder, Gary, xx, 8, 9, 38, 78
Solomon, Carl, 11
Sometimes a Great Notion (Kesey), x
Spengler, Oswald, 4
Stein, Gertrude, *Melanctha*, 65
Stern, Gerd, 34, 54
Sterne, Laurence, 88
Stock, Robert, 9
Subterraneans, The (MacDougall), 21, 85
Summer of the Beautiful White Horse, The (Saroyan), 66
System and Dialectics of Art (Graham), xvii

Tallmer, Jerry, xii–xiii
Tao, 8
Temple of Gold (Goldman), 93
Theotocopuli, Dominico (El Greco), 46

Thoreau, Henry David, 34, 38, 76
Tropic of Cancer (Miller), 24
Twain, Mark, 54, 88
Twardowicz, Stanley, xv–xvi

Uhl, Dave, 79
Ulysses (Joyce), 48

Van Doren, Mark, 28, 73
Van Gogh, Vincent, 46
Vidor, King, *The Champ*, 93
Village Voice, xii
Villon, François, 38, 48

Wald, Jerry, 21
Wallace, Mike, xiii, 3–6
Wechsler, James, 15, 26, 31, 34
Welles, Orson, *Citizen Kane*, xiii–xiv, 26
Whalen, Philip, xx, 8, 9, 17, 78, 79
White, Ed, 35
White Dove Review, 52
Whitman, Walt, xvi, 34, 38
Wilbur, Richard, 63
Williams, Tennessee, 62
Wingate, John, *Nightbeat*, xii
Wolfe, Thomas, xvi, 27, 54, 66, 76

Yeats, William Butler, 56

Zsedely, Miklos, xv